Charles W. Sisson

The ABC of Iron

Charles W. Sisson

The ABC of Iron

ISBN/EAN: 9783337176624

Printed in Europe, USA, Canada, Australia, Japan

Cover: Foto ©Andreas Hilbeck / pixelio.de

More available books at **www.hansebooks.com**

THE
A B C OF IRON

BY
CHAS. W. SISSON.

LOUISVILLE, KY.:
PRESS OF THE COURIER-JOURNAL JOB PRINTING CO.
1893

CONTENTS.

IRON—WHAT IS IT?
A description of the metal and its uses, showing in what combinations it is found and the principal sources.

PIG IRON.
An account of the blast furnace process by which the ores are reduced to pig iron.

CONSTITUENTS OF IRON.
A description of the elements in pig metal which influence cast iron. Described in chapters on
CARBON IN CAST IRON.   PHOSPHORUS IN CAST IRON.
SILICON IN CAST IRON.   MANGANESE IN CAST IRON.
SULPHUR IN CAST IRON.

NUMBERING OF PIG IRON.
Showing the character and analysis of different grades of pig iron, appearance of fracture and the uses to which the several grades are adapted.

GRADING OF IRON.
Should it be by analysis or by fracture?

HOW TO REDUCE COST OF MIXTURE.

STEEL.

PHYSICAL PROPERTIES OF METALS DEFINED.
Table of shrinkage of castings. Weights of castings from patterns, etc.

STATISTICS.
Showing the varieties and production of iron ore, pig iron, pig iron and steel products, railroad mileage and equipment, etc., etc., etc.

EARLY HISTORY AND MANUFACTURE OF IRON.
Brief history of the manufacture and uses of iron from earliest times, being principally extracts from Mr. James M. Swank's " HISTORY OF IRON IN ALL AGES."

INTRODUCTORY.

There is nothing so essential for a foundryman to understand as the action which the different elements in pig iron have on his product. Manufacturers now realize that pig iron is not a simple substance, but is in reality an alloy compound of a number of elements very dissimilar ; that its physical characteristics, strength, elasticity, etc., depend upon the percentages of these elements.

Greater knowledge is being sought concerning the chemical questions involved in foundry practice, and as this knowledge is resulting in the production of better and cheaper material, it becomes necessary for the foundryman who would successfully meet competition to study this well. No foundryman can afford to be ignorant of the nature and properties of iron if he expects to overcome the numerous emergencies that beset every melter of pig iron.

The increasing inquiries on these subjects suggested the publication of this book.

Learned discussions are had on these subjects before societies and mechanical institutions, and papers are written on special subjects which are reproduced in piece-meal in our trade papers and journals. Only few, however, have the opportunity or can afford to attend the meetings of these societies, and the majority do not get to see their transactions published.

There are very valuable works published on the metallurgy of iron and steel, but they are voluminous and technical, and for this reason very discouraging for a beginner. The author has endeavored in the A B C of Iron, to place before the public such information as all foundrymen should possess, in a plain, condensed form, hoping that

INTRODUCTORY.

those who read it will be assisted in their desire to master their business.

The chapters relating to *Constituents of Iron* are made up of gleanings from the writings and publications by authorities on these subjects, and from personal investigation. Except where extended quotations are given, no mention is made of the authority, for the reason that often it became necessary to change the language to have it simple and readily understood.

The author is indebted for information to Howe's "Metallurgy of Steel;" the papers of Mr. W. J. Keep, of the Michigan Stove Company; to Major Edward Doud, C. E., Port Henry, New York; to "The Journal of the Iron and Steel Institute;" Bloxam's Chemistry, numerous other works, and to practical foundrymen.

Beside the chapters relating to the chemical qualities of iron and the source of supply and process by which the ores are reduced to pig iron, the other contents are inserted as being of value and interest.

The statistics compiled from undoubted authority, will be a revelation to many, showing the magnitude and diversity of the iron industry of this country.

IRON—WHAT IS IT?

Iron is a metal. Bloxam tells us that "a metal is an element capable of forming a base by combining with oxygen." These compounds of elements with oxygen are called oxides. The Latin word for iron is *ferum*, and the chemical symbol for it is *Fe*. The oxides of iron are spoken of as ferric oxide, or ferrous oxides, the termination of *ous* signifying that there is a less proportion of oxygen.

Iron is found in almost all forms of rock, clay and earth, and its presence is shown by their colors, iron being one of the commonest of natural mineral coloring ingredients. We find it in small proportions in plants and in larger quantities in the bodies of animals, especially in the blood, which is said to contain about 0.5 per cent. of iron, imparting its color.

Except in the case of meteorites, large metallic masses which occasionally fall to the earth, sometimes of enormous size and of unknown origin, iron is not found in the metallic state.

The chief forms of combination in which iron is found available as sources of the metal, are in the different varieties of the ores of iron. By ores of iron we mean those mineral masses or beds which contain sufficient metal to justify smelting. Ores of iron are not considered rich unless they contain 50 per cent. of metal, and those containing less than 30 per cent. are rarely smelted.

There are many varieties of iron ore, but they are generally classified under four general divisions, viz.: red hematite, brown hematite, magnetite, and carbonate ores, and in quantity mined rank in the order named. The production of red hematite in 1890, according to the census for that year, was $66\frac{2}{3}$ per cent. of all the ore mined; the quantity of magnetite and brown hematite being about equal, or 16 per cent. each of the total, while the carbonates were only about $2\frac{1}{3}$ per cent. of the whole product. A table showing the production of the several varieties mined in each State during 1890, will be found in these pages. These ores all contain impurities such as sulphur, phosphorus, etc., which have great influence on the quality of the iron and determine, to a great extent, the value of the ores.

The ores of iron are used for flux in smelting furnaces producing precious metals, and for the manufacture of paints. It is also used as a fix, lining for heating and puddling furnaces; but the principal use to which they are put is the production of pig iron by smelting the ores in blast furnaces. We will describe briefly this process in the succeeding chapter.

The high position which iron occupies among the useful metals is owing to a combination of valuable qualities not found in any other metal. We find in Bloxam's Chemistry, the following description:

"Although possessing nearly twice as great tenacity or strength as the strongest of the other metals commonly used in the metallic state, it is yet one of the lightest, and is, therefore, particularly well adapted for the construction of bridges and large edifices, as well as for ships and carriages. It is the least yielding or malleable of the metals in common use, and can, therefore, be relied upon for a rigid support; and yet its ductility is such that it admits of being rolled into the thinnest sheets and drawn into the finest wire, the strength of which is so great that a wire of 1-10 inch in diameter is able to sustain 705 pounds, while a similar wire of copper, which stands next in order of tenacity, will not support more than 385 pounds. It is, with the exception of platinum, the least fusible of useful metals and therefore applicable to the construction of fire-grates and furnaces.

"Its qualifications are not all dependent on its physical properties, for it not only enters into a great number of compounds which are of the utmost use in the arts, but its chemical relations to one of the metallic elements, carbon, are such that the addition of a small quantity of this element converts iron into *steel* far surpassing iron in the valuable properties of hardness and elasticity, whereas a larger quantity of carbon gives rise to *cast iron*, the greater fusibility of which permits it to be molded into vessels and shapes which could not be produced by forging." Perhaps the finest description of iron is found in *Ure's Dictionary of Arts, Manufactures and Mines:*

"Every person knows the manifold uses of this truly precious metal. It is capable of being cast into molds of any form; of being drawn out into wires of any desired strength or fineness; of being extended into plates or sheets; of being bent in every direction; of being sharpened, hardened and softened at pleasure.

"Iron accommodates itself to all our wants, our desires and even our caprices. It is equally serviceable to the arts, the sciences, to agriculture and war. The same ore furnishes the sword, the ploughshare, the scythe, the pruning hook, the needle, the graver, the spring of a watch or of a carriage, the chisel, the chain, the anchor, the compass, the cannon and the bomb. It is a medicine of much virtue, and the only metal friendly to the human frame."

What we have to deal with particularly in this book is the product of the blast furnace—*pig iron*. Five elements enter into all pig iron, in a greater or less degree, and in some varieties are found tungsten, and chromium, and also copper, but with these we have rarely to deal.

After a brief account of the process by which the ores are reduced to pig iron, we will consider, in the order named, the effect these five elements—*carbon, silicon, phosphorus, manganese* and *sulphur*—have upon castings made from pig metal.

PIG IRON.

AN ACCOUNT OF THE BLAST FURNACE PROCESS BY WHICH THE ORES ARE REDUCED TO PIG IRON.

The modern blast furnace is supposed to have originated in the Rhine provinces about the beginning of the fourteenth century, but whether in France, Germany or Belgium is not clear. One hundred years later, in 1409, there was a blast furnace in the valley of Massavaux, in France, and it is claimed by Landrin that there were many blast furnaces in France about 1450. The exact date of the erection of the first blast furnace in England is unknown, but it was along in the fifteenth century. The first attempt to make pig iron in the United States was in 1645, at Lynn, Massachusetts. We see, therefore, that, although iron melted by charcoal in the old Catalan forges was used many hundreds of years ago, cast iron or pig iron is of comparative recent origin, and may be said is yet in its infancy.

In the reduction of the ores the fuel may be charcoal, coke, block coal or anthracite coal. Charcoal is freer from impurities than any of the fuels and has been used from the earliest times. Experiments were begun in 1630 with coal and coke, but it was not until 1735 that any degree of success was attained. The first successful blast with coke as fuel was made by Abraham Darby, of Shropshire, at his furnace at Coalbrookdale, England, in the year 1735. The first successful manufacture of pig iron with anthracite coal was by George Crane, an Englishman, at Yniscedirin, in Wales, in 1837. The blast used in furnaces was cold, until 1825, when James Beaumont, of Scotland, invented the hot blast now in general use all over the world. In order to separate the extraneous matter usually contained in a furnace charge of ore and reducing agent, certain materials must be added to form *slags*. These materials are known as *fluxes*. Limestone constitutes the bulk of fluxing used by the blast furnace. The slags of a blast furnace are its refuse, and are formed by a combination of silica with the earths and metallic oxides. They are used, if not too glassy, for macadamizing roads; it makes an excellent railroad ballast, as the mass is very permeable and keeps the sleepers dry. It is also used in making brick and cement.

It is not within the province of this book to give an elaborate or detailed description of the blast furnace, but we will briefly describe, without technicalities, how iron is separated from its ores.

Strictly pure iron ore is metallic iron and oxygen in chemical union in fixed and known proportions; the most common being that of peroxide, which is 70 per cent. of iron to 30 per cent. of oxygen by weight.

Iron ores, as mined, consist of various combinations of iron, oxygen, phosphorus, sulphur, carbonate of lime, carbonate of magnesia, silica, alumina, and sometimes water, manganese, titanic acid, etc.

It is the office of the blast furnace to separate the iron from the other materials. Since chemically pure iron is not used in the arts, such is not sought, nor could it be produced in the blast furnace. Commercial pig iron usually contains 92 to 94 per cent. of pure iron and 6 to 8 per cent. of impurities.

The presence or absence of these impurities in varying proportions give to pig iron its varying characteristics, suiting it to widely varying uses. Upon the proper composition of the impurities depends the grade and value of the pigs.

The highest skill of the iron master is exerted to secure the best possible composition, varying the composition to suit the various uses of his patrons.

The chief components of the impurities are carbon, silicon, phosphorus, sulphur and manganese.

The reduction of the oxide of iron by withdrawing the oxygen, the simultaneous carburisation of the resultant metal and the fluxing of the various earths entering the furnace with the oxide of iron and carbon, are accomplished by the use of the laws of chemical affinities. This use may be empirical or intelligent. The former was the method of the past, sometimes even now disastrously lingering in the lap of the present. The latter is alone in accord with the spirit of to-day, and is soon to be the sole method of the future. These affinities are absolute and positive, and the skillful furnace manager handles them in full confidence, dividing, adding and subtracting as an accountant does his figures.

All solid materials enter the furnace at the top in carefully considered mixtures, determined by analyses to conform to fixed chemical laws. The air equaling or exceeding the combined weight of the solid materials alone, enters near the bottom. The furnace being full and in action, is found to divide into the following zones : Beginning at the bottom we have first the hearth, which is for receiving and holding the liquid mass until convenient intervals for tapping or drawing out. Very little chemical action occurs here. The molten mass quietly rests and the iron separates from the slag by specific gravity. Next comes the zone of gassification. Into this zone is introduced the blast, previously heated to a temperature of 900 to 1,500° Fah., and is driven in under a pressure of five to ten pounds per square inch, and at the rate of three and one-quarter to six tons for each ton of iron made.

The oxygen of the blast coming into direct contact with the incandescent carbon of the fuel, gassification of the carbon rapidly follows, so rapidly indeed that each atom of carbon takes from the air the smallest amount of oxygen necessary for gassification. That is, one atom of oxygen for each atom of carbon. This action is not confined to the oxygen of the air; it extends to any other oxygen available.

Next above the zone of gassification is the zone of fusion, in which chiefly occurs the reduction of the solids, excepting ash of the fuel, to liquids. Above the zone of fusion is the zone of reduction and carbon impregnation. This should occupy a very large part of the body of the furnace.

Thus, the furnace is divided into three zones, which, however, have no definite limits, but insensibly merge one into the other. Nor is it to be understood that the offices attributed to these zones severally is confined within them.

Perhaps nine-tenths of the carbon is volatilized in the zone of gassification and the balance in the zone of reduction, to which is added the oxygen from the ore and the carbonic acid from the limestone, chiefly in the zone of reduction, the furnace producing gas throughout its entire height.

Nor is fusion confined to the so-called zone of fusion, but may and does frequently extend well into the zone of gassification, and it is known that reduction is not completed and the last of the oxygen does not leave the ore until it is well into the zone of fusion.

The gasses leave the zone of combustion, that is gassification at a temperature of 3,500 to 4,000° Fah. As they ascend the heat is transferred to the descending materials to such an extent that the gasses pass out of the top of the furnace with only 300 to 500° Fah. As the escaping gas weighs much more than the materials charged, and as their specific heat does not materially differ, the gas itself could impart sufficient sensible heat to raise the stock to the hearth temperature were the absorptions and generations of heat due to intervening chemical reactions equal.

As it is, however, it will be seen how perfectly a furnace acts as a regenerator, and how small a heat-waste there may be in a furnace well conducted. Beginning at the zone of gassification and ascending through the furnace we find the descending materials always just a little lower in temperature than the ascending column of gas at each successive stage ; presenting by far the most favorable conditions for heat transfer, where the successive lowering of the gas temperature is met by still cooler materials to further reduce the waste, and even in the most rapid furnace-driving this valuable conservation of heat is not over-hastened for the best and ultimate economy, for at least several hours must elapse while each particle of the stock is descending to the hearth.

Following the ores as they enter the furnace, they are first dried and heated by meeting the hot gases. As soon as they have reached a sufficient temperature the ore begins to part with its oxygen to the carbonic oxide forming carbonic acid. Carbonic acid is also eliminated from the limestone, and sometimes from the ores, and

PIG IRON.

many associations and desociations occur not necessary to trace in this article.

As the descending ore becomes hotter the action becomes more rapid until the most favorable temperature for reduction by the gases is reached and passed, when it proceeds more slowly and is supposed to be finally completed by contact with intensely hot solid carbon. That which was ore no longer exists as ore. Its two constituents, which, in chemical union, made it oxide of iron, have been separated, the oxygen expelled from the top of the furnace while the iron in minute particles, having taken up about 4 per cent. of its own weight of carbon, is found changed from oxide of iron to carbide of iron, and is intermingled with the earths and other material. It remains to separate the iron from the earths and put it into form for convenient handling. To do this the entire mass is fused and falls into the hearth. To secure a fusion of its earths a process termed fluxing is resorted to, based on the premise that no single earth, if pure, will melt in the temperatures ordinarily found in the blast furnace, which, while not strictly true, is sufficiently so for present purposes.

The earths usually entering the furnace are either acid or basic, these two having a strong affinity for each other, and when brought together in proper proportions and into the presence of the high heat found in the fusing iron, readily liquify and fall with the liquid iron into the hearth, where by the difference in their specific gravity, they separate, the slag floating on top of the iron.

The space allotted to this article will not admit of an extended review of methods in use for the control in kind and quantity of the various impurities entering into the pigs.

It is sufficient to say that nearly all of the phosphorus entering the furnace is found in the iron leaving it, and it is contrary to the theory of the blast furnace that any of it can be eliminated. Its effect is to make the iron cold-short.

By judicious fluxing and management a limited amount of sulphur charged into the furnace may be discharged with the slag, the iron absorbing but traces of this objectionable alloy. The effect of this sulphur upon the iron is to make it red-short, and every effort of the manager should be directed toward its elimination.

The percentage of silicon is controlled by the temperature in the zone of combustion and the character of the flux.

The intensity of the heat required to decompose oxide of silicon is such that it is impossible to conceive that silicon can be obtained anywhere in the blast furnace except in the foci of intense heat near each blow pipe (Bell), therefore, the oxide of silicon must be brought into these foci. The ash of the fuel is so brought in and being in part silica, it answers the requirement.

PIG IRON.

When the fuel is high in silica the production of silicon is facilitated.

Likewise, by reason of inadequate fluxing or other cause, portions of the silica of the ore and limestone may find their way into these limited areas of intense heat and contribute silicon.

Carbon, as has been stated, combines with iron as the oxygen leaves it to the extent of about 4 per cent. of its weight.

This has made blast furnacing possible, as the combination is fused at a much lower temperature than malleable iron and within that generated in the process, so that a liquid manageable metal is produced which may be drawn from the hearth and molded into merchantable form.

Carbon exists in pig iron as graphitic and combined, and the relative proportions of each will largely control the grade. To produce iron high in graphite the furnace must be in a healthy condition, so that the materials shall descend evenly and regularly, and the reducing gas as it ascends shall come in contact with and reduce all of the ore before fusion. A comparatively light burden favors the production of an increased percentage of the reducing gas, and so favors perfect reduction and also carbon deposition.

CONSTITUENTS OF IRON.

Before describing these constituents and their effects we would call attention to Professor Turner's statement concerning cast iron, which it will be well to remember:

First: Pure cast iron, *i. e.*, iron and carbon only, even if attainable, would not be the most suitable material for use in the foundry.

Second: That cast iron containing excessive amounts of other constituents is equally unsuitable for foundry purposes.

Third: That the ill-effects of one constituent can, at best, be only imperfectly neutralized by the addition of another constituent.

Fourth: That there is a suitable proportion for each constituent present in cast iron. This proportion depends upon the character of the product which is desired, and upon the proportion of other elements present.

Fifth: (More properly coming under head of Silicon) That variations in the proportion of silicon afford a trustworthy and inexpensive means of producing a cast iron of any required mechanical character which is possible with the material employed.

CARBON IN CAST IRON.

Carbon assumes a greater number of aspects than any of the elements we deal with in connection with iron. We find it colorless and transparent in the diamond; opaque, black and partly metallic in graphite or black lead; dull and porous in wood charcoal, and under still other conditions in anthracite, coke and gas carbon. Carbon exerts the most vital influence upon the character of pig iron of all the elements.

The different proportions of carbon held in chemical composition in iron determines whether the material is crude or cast iron, steel, or bar or malleable iron; cast iron containing more than steel and steel more than malleable iron, which last ought to be pure metal, a point of perfection rarely reached. It is impossible to assign the limits between these three forms of iron, or their relative proportions of carbon, with entire precision, for bar iron passes into steel by insensible gradations, and steel and cast iron make such mutual transitions as to render it difficult to define where the former commences and the latter ceases to exist. In fact, some steels may be called crude iron and some cast irons may be classed among steels. Carbon affects the color, strength, hardness and fusibility of cast iron. It exists in pig iron in two distinct forms, the combined and the graphitic or free carbon, and upon the relative proportion of each in a great measure depends the character of the metal.

The "total carbon" is always equal to the combined, plus the graphitic. Graphitic carbon occurs almost exclusively in gray pig iron (foundry irons) in the form of dark thin flakes, varying much in size and intersecting the small particles of iron. Its influence is to make iron softer and tougher, but weaker and less tenaceous than if it existed in the form of combined carbon. Carbon combines with iron up to about 4.63 per cent., and the amount that will be taken up is dependent chiefly upon the percentage of silicon, sulphur and manganese present; silicon and sulphur lowering the amount of carbon, while manganese raises the point of saturation. Phosphorus does not seem to have any effect upon the carbon. Professor Turner, of Mason College, Birmingham, England, has shown that the strength of cast iron depends upon, first, the amount of weakening impurities present, and second, the proportion existing between the combined and graphitic carbon in cast iron. He says that as the tendency of combined carbon is to increase hardness and brittleness, and that of graphitic to make the iron soft, malleable and tough, too much of either form is a disadvantage.

In the chapter on silicon, we will show that by a judicious use of silicon this proportion can be regulated.

Cast iron, when free from manganese, can not hold more than 4.50 per cent. of carbon, and 3.50 per cent. is about as much as is ever present; but as manganese increases, carbon increases also, until we find it in Spiegel as high as 6 per cent. This effect or capacity to hold carbon is peculiar to manganese.

Castings of iron alone or of iron and carbon will always be white and the carbon will always be combined. The grayness of cast iron depends upon the percentage of silicon present. White iron may result from the following four conditions: first, chilling; second, high sulphur; third, low silicon; fourth, high manganese.

SILICON IN CAST IRON.

Next to carbon, silicon is the commonest and most abundant constituent of cast iron.

We have just seen under carbon upon what the strength of cast iron depends, and since strength is the thing most desired, irons having an excess of weakening impurities will not find a market, and what we wish to provide, therefore, is the proper proportion between the combined and the graphitic carbon. Professor Turner, as has also Mr. W. J. Keep, of Detroit, demonstrated that by a judicious use of silicon, this proportioning can be accomplished exactly according to the wish of the founder; an increase of silicon changing combined to graphitic, and *vice versa*. According to Professor Turner, when the founder understands its use, he may soften and toughen or harden and strengthen his iron to suit his requirements. He is careful, however, to advise against the free use of silicon without first understanding when it is needed, for in an iron where the carbon is already graphitic, more silicon may weaken it and make it brittle. It is only within the last five or six years that the usefulness of silicon has been known or recognized. By its use, pig iron and scrap, which, when used alone, are totally unfit for foundry purposes, may be converted into merchantable material.

Silicon has been known as a softening agent, and pig irons that have this element in considerable quantities have been designated as "*softeners*."

For years foundrymen demanded the softeners made in Scotland and from the lean ores of Ohio and Kentucky, and it has only recently become generally known that this softening quality is due to silicon. When this quality in silicon became known, the demand for high silicon increased largely. In 1887, foreign irons containing as high as 10 per cent. silicon were imported into the United States. These high silicon irons varying from 7 to 14 per cent. silicon, go under the name of *ferro silicon*. This demand led to the production of ferro-silicon in this country, and the result of comparison made with foreign irons shows the American softener to be the better.

Iron absorbs silicon greedily, uniting with it in all proportions up to at least 30 per cent., and apparently the more readily the higher the temperature, absorbing it even at a red heat when imbedded in sand. In general, silicon diminishes the power of iron to combine with carbon, not only when molten, but more especially at a white heat, thus favoring the formation of graphite during slow cooling. It increases the fusibility and fluidity of iron, lessens the formation of blow holes and reduces shrinkage. It is thought, by the majority, to increase tensile strength slightly.

Pure iron, if it could be made, unlike most of the metals, would have no commercial value, and would be so pliable and inelastic as to possess but little strength.

The effect of silicon on iron is to change the combined carbon into graphitic carbon, or we may express it by saying that it changes white iron to gray iron, the color of the iron varying from gray to black, depending upon the amount of graphite it contains.

A solid casting could not be made with simple iron and carbon, for the carbon would be entirely in the combined state, and the casting would be white, hard and brittle.

Cast iron, therefore, which contains enough silicon to take out the brittleness, and to allow it to make a solid casting, is the strongest composition ordinarily found in natural cast iron. Professor Keep's tests show that a solid casting having its carbon combined, is stronger than one in which the carbon is more graphitic, and he states that "for strength, therefore, we must endeavor to obtain, instead of a perfectly uniform distribution of graphite, a concentration in uniformly distributed minute pockets, around which the iron holding combined carbon may form a lace work; if strength be more important than softness, we will leave the greatest possible quantity of carbon in the combined state that will not cause the iron to be brittle."

The strongest castings are obtained from irons that will produce sound castings with the least amount of silicon.

It should be remembered that when just enough silicon is obtained to produce a sound casting, any addi-

CONSTITUENTS OF IRON. 27

tional amount of silicon to such iron will decrease the strength and cause brittleness.

Silicon by causing carbon to crystallize out as graphite, lessens shrinkage, and shrinkage would be prevented entirely by the swelling out of the graphite, if it was not prevented by the mass of iron about it. It is best always to use irons that contain the proper amount of silicon for the desired quality of casting, for the graphite separates more easily and the shrinkage is less where the pig iron receives its silicon while in the blast furnace, than where the percentage is made up by adding special ferro-silicon.

From 2 per cent. to 5 per cent. of silicon, depending upon other ingredients present, will change all the combined carbon that can be changed. The change to the graphitic reduces hardness and makes the iron soft so that it can be drilled and filed.

When the carbon has become graphitic, the further addition of silicon hardens cast iron. This, however, is produced entirely through its influence on the carbon and not by direct influence of the silicon. We quote from Professor Keep on this subject: "We have seen, however, that a white iron which will invariably give porous and brittle castings can be made solid and strong by the addition of silicon; that a further addition of silicon will turn the iron gray, and that as the grayness increases, the iron will grow weaker; that excessive silicon will again lighten the grain and cause a hard and brittle as well as a very weak iron; that the only softening and shrinkage lessening influence of silicon is exerted during the time when graphite is being produced, and that silicon of itself is not a softener, or a lessener of shrinkage, but through its influence on carbon, and only during a certain stage does it produce these effects."

By its action on the carbon, silicon reduces the chilling capacity of iron.

The loss of silicon from remelting is very slight.

Foundry irons contain from 1 to 5 per cent. of silicon, ferro-silicon 5 to 14 per cent. and castings from 1 to 3 per cent.

It must not be taken from the apparently broad assertion of Professor Turner, or from any of the foregoing, that the founder has in silicon a remedy for all the ills that iron is heir to. The statements are perfectly reliable and proven, but a given percentage of silicon in iron at the present state of general blast furnace practice will not always produce like results. Each of the irons a founder uses will have peculiar tendencies given them in the blast furnace, which will exert their influence when the iron is remelted.

The percentages of manganese, phosphorus and sulphur must be known to regulate the proper proportion of silicon, and only by great care and attention to the composition of his mixture can the foundryman expect to overcome the difficulties that occur daily in the melting of pig iron.

PHOSPHORUS IN CAST IRON.

Pig iron derives its phosphorus chiefly from the phosphates existing in the ore or in the flux. No element of itself weakens cast iron so much as phosphorus when present in any considerable quantity, and for this reason particular attention should be given to the analysis of all irons. It is not an unmixed evil, however, for when present in quantities ranging from $1\frac{1}{4}$ per cent. and less, it has some beneficial effects, for while it can not be said that it really makes iron more fluid, it prolongs the period of fluidity. Its tendency is to render the metal very limpid so that it will take an extremely fine and sharp casting from the most delicate patterns. The famous Berlin castings of reproductions in iron of ancient armor and other ornamental objects are obtained by using iron rich in phosphorus, but it possesses the disadvantage of rendering the metal brittle and unfit for many practical uses. Were it not for its weakening effect it would not be necessary to keep the phosphorus in foundry mixture at less than 1 to $1\frac{1}{4}$ per cent. Mr. Keep, in a series of tests, demonstrates that phosphorus is a lessener of shrinkage, and as phosphorus does not influence carbon, it must be due to direct action of phosphorus. All high phosphorus irons have low shrinkage.

In the blast furnace phosphorus is not effectively volatilized, for any which volatilizes immediately re-condenses. Hence, in the blast furnace and in the cupola all the phosphorus passes into the metal. Hence, the watchfulness necessary to see that pig iron does not contain an excess of this element. Bloxam calls phosphorus the "hereditary disease," because of the great difficulty of removing it from iron.

It is only eliminated by intense heat as in the puddling furnace, where about 90 per cent. can be eliminated, and in the Basic process, where 96 to 99 per cent. may be removed.

Phosphorus causes iron to be what is known as "cold-short," that is, brittle when cold. Howe says: "Phosphorus probably has little effect on the tensile strength under gently applied load; but phosphoric iron is readily broken by jerky, shock-like or vibratory stresses, sometimes when quite trifling—it is treacherous. It sometimes affects iron but slightly, sometimes under apparently like conditions profoundly—it is capricious."

It must not be expected that a given percentage of phosphorus will behave at all times in the same way, for other elements may be present in such a way as to entirely change the results.

The percentage of phosphorus varies in pig iron from a trace to 1½ per cent. Unless great fluidity is desired and strength is not a consideration, the percentage of phosphorus in pig iron for foundry work should be 0.8 per cent. and less.

MANGANESE IN CAST IRON.

Manganese is seldom absent in pig iron, the percentage depending upon the ore used and the temperature of the furnace. Both in its physical and chemical characters it resembles iron very closely. It is generally produced in the blast furnace, and is combined with iron and small percentages of silicon, phosphorus and sulphur. The metal itself has not been applied to any useful purpose, and is of value, commercially, only when combined with iron. It has been made to replace iron to the extent of 85 per cent. If the silicon is under 0.50 per cent. the product will be white. Pig iron containing manganese from about 5 to 30 per cent., with the remainder mostly iron and silicon not high enough to make the product gray, the alloy is called *spiegeleisen*, and the fracture, as its name indicates, will show flat reflecting surfaces.

With manganese 50 per cent. and over, the iron alloy is called *ferro manganese*. The bulk of the ferro manganese used is imported from England and Germany, and contains 80 per cent. manganese.

We quote the following from Howe's Metallurgy of Steel: "There appears to be no limit to the extent to which manganese can combine with iron; the higher the percentage of manganese in the alloy, the higher is the temperature in the blast furnace necessary for its production. Manganese is reduced from its oxides by carbon at a white heat, and the more readily the more metallic iron is present to combine with it.

"It is easily removed from iron by oxidation, being oxidized even by silicon; and partly in this way, partly in others, it restrains the oxidation of the iron while sometimes restraining, sometimes permitting, the oxidation of the other elements combined with it. Its presence increases the power of carbon to combine with iron at high temperature (say 1400° C.) and restrains its separation as graphite at lower ones."

Manganese assists in the prevention of blow-holes. It bodily removes sulphur from cast iron and thus prevents hot-shortness. It does not counteract cold-shortness caused by phosphorus. In a number of tests Mr. Keep shows that manganese increases the shrinkage of cast iron, and he states that "a high shrinkage caused by manganese is independent of carbon and can not be taken out without removing the manganese. As shrinkage varies with the size of the casting and produces internal stress within the casting, this question is of vital importance to the foundryman. The less shrinkage in the iron, the less the danger from cracks."

Hardness is another important consideration with the founder. An increase of 1 per cent. of manganese has increased the hardness 40 per cent. Mr. Keep's tests show that manganese does not increase chill. If, however, a hard chill is required, manganese gives it by adding hardness to the whole casting. This hardness is

CONSTITUENTS OF IRON. 33

due to the hardness of manganese itself and not because more of the carbon has taken the combined form. In trying to make soft castings with low shrinkage, avoid manganese. The amount of manganese varies in pig iron from a trace to 2 per cent. On account of its tendency to make iron hard and brittle, it can only be tolerated in very strong castings, and even then the percentage should be under 0.75 per cent., and should not exceed 0.5 per cent. in foundry irons. Much of the manganese that is present in a pig iron will escape in the slag during remelting in the cupola, and in so doing benefit the iron by carrying off sulphur which has been brought in with the fuel.

SULPHUR IN CAST IRON.

Sulphur is without doubt the most deleterious substance found in pig iron. The other elements all produce effects which may be beneficial for certain purposes, but sulphur is the enemy dreaded by all, on account of its affinity for iron, combining with it at a low temperature. Sulphur unites with iron, probably in all proportions, up to 53.3 per cent., being readily absorbed from many sources. It causes iron to be what is known as "*red-short*," that is, brittle when hot. It makes iron hard and white, though this may be accounted for partly by its causing iron to retain its carbon in the combined state. It increases the fusibility of cast iron, but makes it thick and sluggish when molten, and gives rise to blow holes during its solidification.

The presence of sulphur in pig iron and in the castings is due mainly to its absorption from the fuel. For this reason close attention should be given the analysis of the fuel used, which, in the case of foundries, is coke. Coke, with sulphur over 0.75 to 0.90 per cent., is not fit for foundry purposes.

Fortunately, sulphur is easily removed by the use of lime, manganese, or fluor spar. Manganese will counteract the red-shortness caused by sulphur and in some cases actually removes sulphur from iron; sometimes by forming some compound rich in sulphur and manganese, which liquidates or separates by gravity, and, perhaps, sometimes by carrying oxygen to the sulphur.

Silicon expels sulphur from iron to a certain limited extent, but not enough to be of importance commercially. Lime is, perhaps, more generally used than any alkali for removing sulphur. Not a few use fluor spar, and this is found to be an excellent desulphurizing agent when its use is understood.

NUMBERING OF IRON.

The present mode of selling pig iron is by the appearance of the fracture of the pig metal when broken, and the producing districts have different classifications for their metal. Some of these districts have three or four grades only, while others have as many as eight or ten, and we have the card of a charcoal iron company that designates fourteen grades.

This multiplicity of grades and the variations of the grading in different sections of the country will always be confusing, and must soon lead to the sale and purchase of pig iron by analysis. We give further reasons for the change to this basis in the chapter devoted to the subject of grading.

For all practical purposes we can resolve the numerous classifications to about the following grades:

ANTHRACITE AND COKE.

Nos. 1, 2 and 3 Foundry; Grey Forge; Mottled and White.

CHARCOAL.

Nos. 1, 2, 3 and 5 Foundry; and Nos. 1, 2, 3, 4, 5, 6 and 7 Car-wheel.

Besides these, we have in the South the soft and

silvery irons, and in Ohio the silicized irons containing from 4 to 10 per cent. of silicon, both used to soften other irons and make them run fluid. In addition we have the low phosphorus and sulphur irons used in the open hearth and Bessemer process for making steel, and the low silicon and high phosphorus irons used in the basic process.

The carbon in pig iron is what enables the eye to distinguish the different grades; the softest, grayest iron having almost all the carbon in the graphitic or uncombined state, while the hard and white irons have it nearly or wholly combined.

As we have already seen, the color, strength, hardness, etc., of cast iron depend upon the relative proportions of these two forms of carbon, varied, of course, by the influence of silicon, sulphur, manganese and phosphorus, which are always present to a greater or less extent.

ANTHRACITE AND COKE IRONS.

No. 1 Foundry is the darkest of the numbers as well as the softest, as it contains the most graphitic carbon. It is used exclusively in the foundry. In appearance the fracture is dark in color, rough, open grain; tensile strength and elastic limit low; turns soft and tough.

No. 2 Foundry is more generally used in the foundry than any other grade. The grain is not so open and large as No. 1 Foundry, but the iron is harder and stronger, although less tough and more brittle. These two grades, especially No. 1 Foundry, become very liquid when melted, and will run into castings of the frailest and finest structure. The high numbers do not become so liquid when melted as Nos. 1 and 2. Graphitic carbon and silicon are both less in No. 2 than in No. 1.

No. 3 Foundry is used for both mill and foundry purposes. It is much stronger than Nos. 1 and 2, the grain being closer and more compact. It turns hard, is less tough and more brittle than No. 2. The strength for tension seems to reach its limit in this grade. It is less liquid than Nos. 1 and 2 and is, therefore, better adapted to heavy castings. The percentages of graphitic carbon and silicon are smaller and combined carbon larger than in No. 2.

Grey Forge iron is midway between No. 3 Foundry and Mottled, and is used principally in rolling mills. It turns hard and is weaker than No. 3, color lighter and verging into a white background; grain very close. Graphitic carbon and silicon in smaller proportion than in No. 3, and combined carbon in larger.

Mottled: Except in the case of heavy castings requiring great strength and closeness of grain, where it is mixed with other irons, Mottled iron is used exclusively for puddling purposes. Turns with great difficulty, less tough and more brittle than Grey Forge. Graphitic carbon and silicon lower than in Grey Forge and combined carbon higher.

NUMBERING OF IRON.

White: It is only when a furnace is working badly that this grade is produced. It has a smooth, white fracture, no grain and is used exclusively in a rolling-mill; tensile strength and elastic limit very low; too hard to turn or drill, as the carbon in this grade is about all in the combined state.

No. 1 Soft, in grain is similar to 1 and 2 Foundry, lighter in color, quite soft and fluid with fair strength.

No. 2 Soft, runs between a 2 and 3 Foundry, except that it is light in color and is higher in both graphitic carbon and silicon. These irons, together with silvery irons, which are light in color and high in graphitic carbon and silicon, are used, as the name would indicate, for mixing with stronger and closer grained iron to make them soft and run fluid.

CHARCOAL IRONS.

Foundry irons made from charcoal are considerably stronger, and, because of the fuel, are much freer from impurities than irons made from coke or coal. The grain of charcoal irons of the same numbers as coke runs closer. They are used in foundries where great strength is required in castings.

CAR WHEEL IRONS.

No. 1 is the softest grade, of which very little is used. It will not chill, and is used for ordinary castings.

No. 2 is produced in considerable quantities. It is

closer in grain, is generally free from chill, is used for making malleable castings from furnaces and in remelting old wheels for a softener.

No. 3 is a harder iron and chills from one-quarter to three-quarters of an inch; is much used with softer irons in manufacturing car wheels.

No. 4 is a still harder iron and will chill from three-quarters to one and one-quarter inches. This grade is used almost entirely for car wheel purposes.

No. 5 is about half white in the pig, and will chill from one and one-quarter to one and three-quarter inches.

Nos. 6 and 7 are white iron.

Nos. 5, 6 and 7 are mixed with softer irons in car wheel mixtures, and are also used in making chilled rolls.

There does not seem to be any standard governing furnaces, so far as the analysis of the different grades are concerned. This is accounted for by the variations of the constituents in iron ores as well as the character of fuel used, which make it impossible to establish an analysis that would be accepted by all furnaces as a standard.

It would be possible to regulate the graphitic carbon and the silicon, which the grades should contain, but not the other impurities.

NUMBERING OF IRON.

We give analyses showing about the average proportions of the elements found in the several grades:

ANALYSES.

	No. 1 F'dry.	No. 2 F'dry.	No. 3 F'dry.	Grey Forge.	Mottled.	White.	Soft.	Silvery.
Iron	92.46	93.04	93.93	94.01	93.98	94.64	91.98	90.68
Graphitic Carbon	3.54	3.01	2.50	2.00	1.90	...	3.65	3.00
Combined Carbon	.14	.28	.75	1.80	1.95	3.65	.05	.06
Silicon	2.80	2.55	1.95	1.00	.91	.40	3.40	5.25
Phosphorus	.75	.70	.30	.65	.50	.25	.50	.75
Sulphur	.01	.02	.02	.02	.02	.10	.02	.01
Manganese	.30	.40	.55	.52	.74	.96	.40	.25

The Lake Superior and other Northern irons having a tendency to red-shortness, and the Southern irons having a tendency to cold-shortness, has resulted in the mixing of the irons from the different sections to very great advantage.

GRADING OF IRON.
SHOULD IT BE BY ANALYSIS OR FRACTURE?

We have just seen in the chapter on the "Numbering of Iron" that pig iron is graded according to the fracture, and how confusing and unsatisfactory this system is. This custom of grading has been in vogue so long that many have grown to think it is the only way to determine the character of the iron; but while the eye is a fair guide in fixing the grade, it is not possible to tell the percentages of the impurities in the iron from the appearance of the fracture, consequently the system is deceptive.

On the other hand if iron is graded by analysis, the amount of the percentages is determined accurately, and if the effect of these elements is known, the foundryman is enabled to select only such iron as will benefit his mixture.

There are a great many foundrymen that will not believe chemical knowledge can be of any advantage to them in making a selection of irons for their mixtures. The knowledge can surely do no harm, but will, on the contrary, accomplish results that would have been impossible with simply a knowledge of the fractures.

GRADING OF IRON. 43

We do not believe any property of iron can be determined by its fracture except the condition of the carbon, whether it be in the graphitic or combined state. Sulphur and phosphorus, and even manganese could be present in such quantities as to injure the iron for many uses, and yet there is nothing in the fracture to indicate it. Since then these injurious elements which so greatly affect the quality or character of their product can not be detected by the appearance of the fracture, why insist upon a system in vogue hundreds of years ago when the effects of the elements were unknown, and iron was considered a simple element, and which is the cause often of inferior castings and heavy loss?

All furnacemen know that the fracture can not always be relied on, and that, frequently, iron graded under the present system as No. 2, or even No. 3 Foundry, will run as soft on remelting as a No. 1, but no foundryman could be persuaded to accept it for a No. 1 from appearance of fracture. One furnaceman interviewed on this subject, said, " we can make pig iron that by fracture is as beautiful a No. 1 as any one cares to see, yet on a remelt in a cupola it will run nearly white, like a No. 5."

It will be seen, therefore, that no one can tell how pig iron is going to melt from the appearance of the fracture of that pig iron.

The furnacemen are much in advance of the foundrymen and other consumers of pig iron in the chemistry of iron. They have learned that pure iron, like pure gold, is always the same thing physically and chemically, no matter from what source it comes, and that its different characteristics are imparted to it by and dependent upon the percentages of these elements in combination with it. Through study and the discussion of the chemistry of iron, the furnacemen have in the last few years made great improvement in their practice and in the uniformity of their product. To inquiry made of some thirty manufacturers of pig iron as to whether they could make pig iron of such uniformity as would enable them to sell by analysis rather than by fracture, only affirmative answers were received and the hope expressed that this basis would soon be adopted. Some furnaces have already adopted it with satisfactory results. There is no reason why a chemist should not tell the physical qualities of pig iron from an analysis as easily and accurately as the naturalist can tell the genus of an animal from an examination of a single bone.

Among the founders, however, little attention has been paid to the chemistry of iron, but when they have once seen the great advantage to them of this basis of grading, we do not hesitate to say that iron will be purchased on no other basis than that of analysis. There is still much for the chemist to solve before many of the apparent inconsistencies of analysis will be fully understood; but with a better knowledge on the part of the founder of the effect of the elements on his mixture, will come the demand for iron having a guaranteed percentage of certain elements for the required work. The success of the steel industry is largely due to the scientific attention bestowed upon the chemistry of steel and its manufacture has been carried, on this account, to a fine degree of perfection. There is no reason why iron should not reach the same perfection and be sold by analysis as steel is.

We feel that the time is not far distant when all iron must be sold on basis of analysis. It means a common language for both producer and consumer in discussing the qualities or characteristics of an iron. The founder having obtained a mixture suited to his purpose and knowing its constituents, has only to indicate his necessities to have his order filled with a degree of satisfaction not known or possible under the present system, because in the matter of fracture no two furnaces grade exactly alike, and as previously stated, the iron may run much softer or harder than the grade under which the fracture would indicate it should be classed. By analysis the grading can be guaranteed, and only in this way can perfect uniformity be attained.

HOW TO REDUCE COST OF MIXTURE.

The author can do no more than offer a suggestion on this subject. His experience and investigation do not warrant the laying down of any rules or suggesting any formulas that would bring about this result.

The character of work differs so much in foundries that what would be suitable for one might not be for another; and while the mixture would answer several purposes, in the one case it might be an economical one and in the others a very expensive mixture.

It is certain, however, that the foundryman who is ignorant of the ingredients of his mixture can not hope to accomplish much in the direction of cheapening his product. We do not look for a fine composition in literature from a man ignorant of the alphabet, or a fine painting from one who does not know how to draw or mix his colors; no more can we expect the best material at the minimum cost from a man that is not master of his tools, which, with the foundryman, are the constituents of his mixture.

We do not argue that the foundryman must take a course in chemistry; this is not necessary or always practicable. The information to be gathered from the articles in this book on the *"constituents of iron"* are sufficient to show the necessity for attention and study of the subject either from text-books or from publications of reliable authorities. A knowledge of the effects of the elements that enter into his mixture and practical experience with them, will soon enable the founder to leave the traditional mixture for one better suited to his requirements in every particular.

Perhaps he thinks the quantities of injurious elements are so small they can not affect much, either way, the quality of his casting. We need only to point him to the very small quantity of plumbago (carbon) that will change iron into steel, as the best evidence of how profoundly certain elements affect the properties of metals. Such changes may cause the material to be very useful or entirely worthless.

We suggest that when a casting is made that answers all requirements as to strength, etc., that an analysis be made both of the casting and the mixture from which it is made. The former will show the percentages of the ingredients that combine to give him the casting of the qualities desired; and the latter will show what elements are necessary and the impurities permissible in the pig iron to produce the casting.

It is only when the proper percentages are known and the effects of the different elements understood, that a foundryman can begin to experiment successfully. By carefully studying the analyses of the various brands of pig iron offered from different sections of the country, it will no doubt be found that the same result can be accomplished by a combination of irons of the lower and less expensive grades. The object which a founder has to keep in view is to use the cheapest metal consistent with obtaining in the casting the requisite properties for the purpose to which it is to be employed.

We would advise the foundryman to study his requirement; learn for *himself* what elements he needs to give strength, softness, fluidity, etc., to his iron. He will then not be dependent upon the "salesman with a mixture" who, to have him buy his iron, will cause him to try iron not suited to his necessities, often resulting in the loss of hundreds of dollars. A little knowledge on the part of the foundryman will enable him to avoid all this, and to tell before trying an iron whether it is suited to his work, or will do what is claimed for it.

Constant watchfulness, however, is necessary at all times, for because of the present mode of grading iron and the irregularity of blast furnace product in some sections, the producer of pig iron does not always deliver material of exactly uniform character, and the slightest variation of some of the ingredients may be sufficient to change entirely the nature of the castings.

STEEL.

Mr. Swank, in his "Iron in All Ages," speaking of Huntsman's invention for making steel, says: "There have been many other improvements in the manufacture of steel, and more recently there has been a very great relative increase in its production and use as compared with iron, until it has become a hackneyed expression that this is the Age of Steel. While this is true in the sense that steel is replacing iron, it is well to remember that the ancients made steel of excellent quality and that the art of manufacturing it was never lost and has never been neglected. The swords of Damascus and the blades of Toledo bear witness to the skill in the manufacture of steel which existed at an early day in both Asia and Europe. German steel was widely celebrated for its excellence during the middle ages, and steel of the same name and made by the same process still occupies an honorable place among metallurgical products. Even Huntsman's invention of the art of making the finest quality of steel in crucibles, while meritorious in itself, was but the reproduction and amplification in a modern age of a process for manufacturing steel of equal quality which was known to the people of India thousands of years ago."

Because of the wonderfully rapid growth and importance of this industry, we think a brief description of the principal methods of manufacturing steel entirely appropriate. Some of the processes are intricate and elaborate, and we can only attempt here an outline of them. Besides those we shall describe there are a number of other so-called steel processes, but, as a rule, they are untried, and some systems that may in the near future be of practical benefit are not yet worked out.

The oldest system of making steel is the *Crucible System.* By this process most all of the fine grade of steel is made. It consists in cutting up Swedish iron or other low phosphorus irons into small pieces and putting them into covered crucibles, which crucibles are placed in a furnace and permitted to remain there a longer or shorter time, according to the quality of steel to be made. Succeeding this is the *Open Hearth System,* which consists of an open hearth furnace, with a circular bottom, ranging in capacity from five to thirty tons. In these open hearth furnaces, as a rule, the process of making steel consists in melting down primarily a certain proportion of good Bessemer pig iron, low in phosphorus, to form what is called a bath. Into this melted pig iron, or bath, after the iron is thoroughly melted, is thrown scrap steel of various kinds, owing to the quality of steel that is to be made. This system covers a very broad range of steel making, running from the commonest agricultural steel to the finest boiler plates. By some it is believed that the open hearth system will entirely supersede the crucible, but crucible steel is still superior to that produced in other ways.

The great output of steel, however, is made by the different pneumatic processes known as the *Bessemer* and the *Clapp-Griffith* and some other modifications of that system. The Clapp-Griffith process is nothing more or less than the Bessemer process applied to shallower vessels on a smaller scale. The Bessemer system consists in melting Bessemer pig iron under .10 in phosphorus in a cupola and running it into a large vessel known as the *Bessemer Converter.* This converter is so arranged at the bottom that tuyeres, containing a large number of small holes, are placed in the bottom of it and through these tuyeres blast pressure is forced up through the iron in the converter until the proper amount of carbon is burned out of the iron. The proper amount of carbon for the desired quality of steel is then restored by the introduction of spiegeleisen and ferro-manganese into the Bessemer converter. A peculiarity of the process consists in the entire absence of any fuel whatever in converting the already melted cast iron into steel, the carbon and silicon in the iron combining with the oxygen of the atmospheric blast to produce an intensely high temperature. The Bessemer process derives its name from Sir Henry Bessemer, of England, who is generally accredited as being the inventor. He began his experiments in 1854, secured his patents in 1856, but it was not until 1858 that complete success was achieved by him in the conversion of cast iron into cast steel, and his success at this time was due to the assistance of Robert F. Mushet. For, although Mr. Bessemer had discovered that melted cast iron could be decarbonized and desiliconized and rendered malleable by blowing cold air through it at a high pressure, he had been unable to retain or restore the small amount of carbon necessary to produce steel. Mr. Mushet overcame the difficulty by adding to the cast iron that has been decarbonized and desiliconized, from 1 to 5 per cent. of a melted triple compound of iron, carbon and manganese; spiegeleisen being the cheapest form of the compound. Mr. Bessemer's prosperity dated from Mushet's discovery, and he realized something over $5,000,000, while Mr. Mushet died as he lived—a poor man. Mr. Wm. Kelly, who died in Louisville in 1888, claimed to have discovered this process before Mr. Bessemer, and the Commissioner of Patents conceded the justness of his claim. He began his experiments in 1847 at Eddyville, Ky., but failed to apply for patents until 1857, a few months after Sir Henry Bessemer obtained two patents in this country. In 1866 the American patents of Kelly, Bessemer, and Mushet were consolidated, and the growth of the industry in this country dated from that time. The process just described is known as the *Acid* Bessemer process.

The *Basic* Bessemer process is important in that it permits of the use of iron high in phosphorus. The credit for the discovery of the method of eliminating phosphorus is due to two English chemists, Sidney G. Thomas and Percy C. Gilchrist. The process consists in lining the Bessemer converter with dolomite limestone. The phosphorus is eliminated by the action of this dolomite lining.

We do not attempt a description of many so-called processes for making steel. Many of them are impracticable in competition, in a commercial sense, with the processes just described.

Great difficulty was experienced at the beginning of the Bessemer steel industry of this country, in obtaining suitable pig iron and lining material for the converters, many failures occurring in using iron that was not suited for conversion into steel. All difficulties have long been overcome, and this industry has been brought to a higher degree of perfection in the United States than it has attained in any other country. The United States is now not only independent of other countries for its supply of Bessemer pig iron, but it is also the largest producer of Bessemer pig iron in the world.

PHYSICAL PROPERTIES OF METALS DEFINED.

W. C. ROBERTS-AUSTEN.

Density: The density of a metal depends on the intimacy of the contact between the molecules. It is dependent, therefore, on the crystalline structure, and is influenced by the temperature of casting, by the rate of cooling, by the mechanical treatment, and by the purity of the metal. The density of a metal is augmented by wire-drawing, hammering, and any other physical method of treatment in which a compressing stress is employed. Pressure on all sides of a piece of metal increases its density.

Malleability: This is the property of permanently extending in all directions, without rupture, by pressure produced by slow stress or impact. The malleability of a metal is dependent on its purity. Relative malleability may be determined by the degree of thinness of the sheets that can be produced by beating or rolling the metals, without annealing.

Ductility: This is the property that enables metals to be drawn into wire.

Tenacity: This is the property possessed by metals, in varying degrees, of resisting the separation of their molecules by the action of a tensile stress.

Toughness is the property of resisting the separation of the molecules after the limit of elasticity has been passed.

Hardness is the resistance offered by the molecules of a substance to their separation by the penetrating action of another substance.

Brittleness is the sudden interruption of molecular cohesion when the substance is subjected to the action of some extraneous force, such as a blow or a change of temperature. It is largely influenced by the purity of the metal.

Elasticity is the power a body possesses of resuming its original form after the removal of an external force which has produced a change in that form. The point at which the elasticity and the applied stress exactly counterbalance each other, is termed the *Limit of Elasticity*. If the applied stress were then removed, the material acted upon would resume its original form. If, however, the stress were increased, the change in form would become permanent, and *permanent set* would be effected. Within the limit of elasticity a uniform rod of metal lengthens or shortens equally under equal additions of stress. If this were the case beyond that limit, it is obvious that there would be some stress that would stretch the bar to twice the original length, or shorten it to zero. This stress, expressed in pounds or tons for a bar of one inch square cross section, is termed the *Modulus of Elasticity*. In measuring the strength of iron or steel two points have usually to be determined—the limit of elasticity, and the ultimate *tensile strength* or maximum stress the material can sustain without rupture.

TABLE OF SHRINKAGES OF CASTINGS.
OVERMANN.

The following table gives the shrinkages of various kinds of castings:

In locomotive cylinders	$\frac{1}{16}$ inch in a foot.
In pipes	$\frac{1}{8}$ inch in a foot.
Girders, beams, etc.	$\frac{1}{8}$ inch in 15 inches.
Engine beams, connecting-rods	$\frac{1}{8}$ inch in 16 inches.
In large cylinders, say 70 inches diameter, 10 feet stroke, the contraction of diameter is about	$\frac{3}{8}$ inch at top.
Contraction of diameter is about	$\frac{1}{2}$ inch at bottom.
Shrinkage of length is	$\frac{1}{8}$ inch in 16 inches.
In thin brass	$\frac{1}{8}$ inch in 9 inches.
In thick brass	$\frac{1}{8}$ inch in 10 inches.
In zinc	$\frac{1}{16}$ inch in 12 inches.
In lead (according to purity)	$\frac{1}{16}$ to $\frac{1}{16}$ inch in 12 inches.
In copper " " "	$\frac{1}{16}$ to $\frac{1}{32}$ inch in 12 inches.
In tin " " "	$\frac{1}{16}$ to $\frac{1}{32}$ inch in 12 inches.
In silver	about $\frac{1}{8}$ inch in 12 inches.

The above values vary slightly with the shape of the pattern, the amount of ramming, the fluidity and heat of the metal at pouring time, and also with the nature of the mould, whether of dry or green sand, or loam. The practice of a foundry varies somewhat from that of another establishment. The only agreement is in the averages.

WEIGHTS OF CASTINGS FROM PATTERNS.
OVERMANN.

If it be desired to make an approximate guess of the weight of a casting from the pattern at hand, the latter may be weighed, and the corresponding weight of the casting will be found in the following tables. It is evident that account should be taken of the core prints, and battens, and other extraneous parts on the pattern, and that their weights should be deducted.

The first table is from Rose's "Pattern Maker's Assistant," and probably agrees with American practice and woods used for patterns. The second table is of European origin, and discrepancies may be accounted for by the difference of densities of the materials. European woods are generally more dense than the corresponding ones of America.

A PATTERN WEIGHING ONE POUND, MADE OF	WILL WEIGH WHEN CAST IN				
	Cast-iron	Zinc	Copper	Yellow Brass	Gun Metal
	lbs.	lbs.	lbs.	lbs.	lbs.
Mahogany—Nassau	10.7	10.4	12.8	12.2	12.5
" Honduras	12.9	12.7	15.3	14.6	15.
" Spanish	8.5	8.2	10.1	9.7	9.9
Pine—red	12.5	12.1	14.9	14.2	14.6
" white	16.7	16.1	19.8	19.	19.5
" yellow	14.1	13.6	16.7	16.	16.5

58   THE A B C OF IRON.

A PATTERN WEIGHING ONE POUND, MADE OF	WILL WEIGH WHEN CAST IN				
	Cast-iron	Brass	Copper	Bronze	Bell or gun metal	Zinc
Pine or fir	14.	15.8	16.7	16.3	17.1	13.5
Oak	9.	10.1	10.4	10.3	10.9	8.6
Beech	9.7	10.9	11.4	11.3	11.9	9.1
Linden	13.4	15.1	15.7	15.5	16.3	12.9
Pear	10.2	11.5	11.9	11.8	12.4	9.8
Birch	10.6	11.9	12.3	12.2	12.9	10.2
Alder	12.8	14.3	14.9	14.7	15.5	12.2
Mahogany	11.7	13.2	13.7	13.5	14.2	11.2
Brass	0.84	0.95	0.99	0.98	1.	0.81
Tin with ¼ to ⅓ of lead	0.89	1.	1.03	1.03	1.12	0.85
Lead	0.64	0.72	0.74	0.74	0.78	0.61

TABLE

Showing the tenacities and resistances to compression, of various simple metals and alloys.

METALS AND ALLOYS.	Tenacity. A bar of one inch square section, will be torn asunder by	Resistance to Compression. One square inch will be crushed by	Resistance to Torsion.
	Pounds.	Pounds.	
Cast Iron	15,000 to 30,000	86,000 to 100,000	9.0
Copper, Wrought ..	33,000		4.3
Malleable Iron	56,000 to 70,000		10.0
Lead	1,824		1.0
Steel	120,000 to 150,000	200,000 to 250,000	16 to 19
Tin	5,000		1.4
Zinc	9,000		
Common Brass	17,900	10,300	4.6

TO MEND CASTINGS.
BOLLAND.

To MEND HOLES IN CASTINGS.—Sulphur in powder, 1 part; sal-ammoniac in powder, 2 parts; fine iron borings, 80 parts. Make into a thick paste and fill the holes.

NOTE.—These ingredients can be kept separate, and mixed when required.

Sulphur, 2 parts; fine black-lead, 1 part. Melt the sulphur in an iron pan; then add the lead; stir well and pour out. When cool, break into small pieces. A sufficient quantity being placed on the part to be mended can be soldered with a hot iron.

To FILL HOLES IN CASTINGS.—Lead, 9 parts; antimony, 2; and bismuth, 1. Melt together and pour in. (Expands in cooling.)

TESTS TO DETERMINE SULPHUR IN COKE.

1st. Dip in water and allow to dry in air. Sulphur will show in rough spots like iron pyrites.

2nd. Nearly every foundry uses sulphuric acid or oil of vitriol (same thing) in the wood pattern shop. Pour a little of it on a piece of coke, and if it is high in sulphur the odor will be very perceptible.

STATISTICS.

IRON ORES.

The United States Geological Survey divides the iron ores into the following classes :

Red Hematite: Those ores in which the iron is found as an anhydrous sesquioxide, including "specular," "fossil," "micaceous," "martite," "slate iron ores," etc. They range in color from light red to steel gray, and are recognized by a red streak on a test plate.

Brown Hematite: Includes all those ores in which the iron is found as a hydrated sesquioxide, the color ranging from yellow to dark brown and black. This class includes "bog ore," "limonite," "turgite," "goethite," etc., and is recognized by a brown streak on a test plate.

Magnetite: Includes all those ores in which the iron occurs principally as magnetic oxide of iron, viz.: Fe_3O_4. These ores are magnetic and give a black streak.

Carbonate: Comprises ores in which the protoxide of iron is associated with a large percentage of carbonic acid, and includes "black band," "spathic," "siderite," and "clay iron stones." They are generally light gray to brown, sometimes dark brownish red, according to the extent to which they are weathered.

The largest amount of iron ore mined in any year was reached in 1890, when the output was 16,036,043 long tons. In addition to this home production there was imported in 1890, 1,246,830 tons and in 1891, 912,864 tons. The importation came principally from Spain, Cuba and Italy; these countries supplying about 40, 30 and 10 per cent., respectively, of the total importation.

The following groupings of ore-producing mines are made by the Census Bureau for the production of 1889, showing in a marked way the comparatively small areas contributing the great bulk of the supply for that year. The four districts or ranges embraced in the Lake Superior region are none of them of great extent geographically, and if a circle was struck from a center in Lake Superior with a radius of one hundred and thirty-five miles all of the iron ore producing territory of the Lake Superior region would be embraced within one-half of the circle and most of the deposits would be near the periphery. The output of this section was 7,519,614 long tons. A parallelogram sixty miles in length and twenty miles in width would embrace all of the producing mines in the Lake Champlain district of Northern New York, whose output in 1889 aggregated 779,850 long tons. A single locality, namely, Cornwall, in Lebanon county, Pa., contributed 769,020 long tons in 1889. A circle of fifty miles radius, embracing portions of Eastern Alabama and Western Georgia, included mines which in 1889 produced 1,545,066 long tons.

By way of comparison we give the production of the different characters of ore mined during the last three years, and for the years 1890 and 1891 give the production of these varieties by States in the order of their precedence as iron-ore producers. The tables are made up from statistics prepared by Mr. John Birkinbine, special agent for Census Bureau.

Productions of Various Kinds of Iron Ore in 1890 By States.

STATES.	Red Hematite.	Brown Hematite.	Magnetite.	Carbonate.	Total.
Michigan	6,426,077	402,274	313,305	. . . . .	7,141,656
Alabama	1,538,297	359,518	. . . . .	. . . . .	1,897,815
Pennsylvania	143,745	415,779	765,318	36,780	1,361,622
New York	196,035	30,968	945,071	81,319	1,253,393
Wisconsin	784,257	164,708	. . . . .	. . . . .	948,965
Minnesota	891,910	. . . . .	. . . . .	. . . . .	891,910
Virginia	16,212	522,908	4,463	. . . . .	543,583
New Jersey	6,000	. . . .	489,808	. . . . .	495,808
Tennessee	278,076	187,619	. . . . .	. . . . .	465,695
Georgia	69,271	174,817	. . . . .	. . . . .	244,088
Missouri	159,440	22,250	. . . . .	. . . . .	181,690
Ohio	. . . . .	. . . . .	. . . . .	169,088	169,088
Colorado	14,698	99,577	. . . . .	. . . . .	114,275
Montana, Oregon, New Mexico, Utah	3,632	48,000	30,000	. . . . .	81,632
Kentucky	. . . . .	15,685	. . . . .	62,000	77,685
Maryland	. . . . .	23,343	. . . . .	12,314	35,657
Massachusetts	. . . . .	32,934	. . . . .	. . . . .	32,934
Connecticut	. . . . .	26,058	. . . . .	. . . . .	26,058
West Virginia	. . . . .	9,000	. . . . .	16,116	25,116
North Carolina	. . . . .	. . . . .	22,873	. . . . .	22,873
Texas	. . . . .	22,000	. . . . .	. . . . .	22,000
Maine	. . . . .	2,500	. . . . .	. . . . .	2,500
Total	10,527,650	2,559,938	2,570,838	377,617	16,036,043
Percentage of Total	65.65	15.96	16.03	2.36	100

STATISTICS. 63

Productions of Various Kinds of Iron Ore in 1891 By States.

STATES.	Red Hematite.	Brown Hematite.	Magnetite.	Carbonate.	Total.
Michigan	5,445,371	457,507	224,123	. . . .	6,127,001
Alabama	1,524,783	462,047	. . . .	. . . .	1,986,830
Pennsylvania	162,683	363,894	727,299	19,052	1,272,928
New York	153,723	53,152	782,729	27,612	1,017,216
Minnesota	945,105	. . . .	. . . .	. . . .	945,105
Virginia	3,274	653,342	2,300	. . . .	658,916
Wisconsin	527,705	61,776	. . . .	. . . .	589,481
Tennessee	396,883	147,040	. . . .	. . . .	543,923
New Jersey	3,850	3,840	517,922	. . . .	525,612
Georgia	45,027	205,728	. . . .	. . . .	250,755
Colorado	6,940	99,253	4,749	. . . .	110,942
Missouri	99,518	7,431	. . . .	. . . .	106,949
Ohio	. . . .	. . . .	. . . .	104,487	104,487
Kentucky	. . . .	45,111	. . . .	19,978	65,089
Texas	. . . .	51,000	. . . .	. . . .	51,000
Massachusetts	. . . .	47,502	. . . .	. . . .	47,502
New Mexico	. . . .	1,000	38,776	. . . .	39,776
Maryland	. . . .	19,400	. . . .	17,979	37,379
Connecticut	. . . .	30,923	. . . .	. . . .	30,923
Oregon	. . . .	29,018	. . . .	. . . .	29,018
North Carolina	. . . .	. . . .	19,210	. . . .	19,210
Montana	8,536	4,000	. . . .	. . . .	12,536
Utah	4,000	8,000	. . . .	. . . .	12,000
West Virginia	. . . .	6,200	. . . .	. . . .	6,200
Idaho	. . . .	400	. . . .	. . . .	400
Total	9,327,398	2,757,564	2,317,108	189,108	14,591,178
Percentage of Total	63.92	18.90	15.88	1.30	100

Total Production of Iron Ore—1889, 1890 and 1891.

STATES AND TERRITORIES.	1891. Rank	1891. PRODUCTION. Long Tons.	1890. Rank	1890. PRODUCTION. Long Tons.	1889. Rank	1889. PRODUCTION. Long Tons.
Michigan	1	6,127,001	1	7,141,656	1	5,856,169
Alabama	2	1,986,830	2	1,897,815	2	1,570,319
Pennsylvania	3	1,272,928	3	1,361,622	3	1,560,234
New York	4	1,017,216	4	1,253,393	4	1,247,537
Minnesota	5	945,105	6	891,910	5	864,508
Virginia	6	658,916	7	543,583	7	498,154
Wisconsin	7	589,481	5	948,965	6	837,399
Tennessee	8	543,923	9	465,695	8	473,294
New Jersey	9	525,612	8	495,808	9	415,510
Georgia	10	250,755	10	244,088	12	248,020
Colorado	11	110,942	13	114,275	13	109,136
Missouri	12	106,949	11	181,690	10	265,718
Ohio	13	104,487	12	169,088	11	254,294
Montana, Oregon, New Mexico and Utah	14	93,330	14	81,632	14	86,405
Kentucky	15	65,089	15	77,685	15	77,487
Texas	16	51,000	21	22,000	20	13,000
Massachusetts	17	47,502	17	32,934	16	46,242
Maryland	18	37,379	16	35,657	18	29,380
Connecticut	19	30,923	18	26,058	17	29,690
North Carolina	20	19,210	20	22,873	22	10,125
West Virginia	21	6,200	19	25,116	19	13,101
Idaho	22	400	.	. . . .	.	. . . .
Maine	.	. . . .	22	2,500	21	12,319
Total		14,518,041		16,036,043		14,591,178

PRICES OF LAKE SUPERIOR IRON ORE.

With the exception of the Lake Superior district the iron ores mined are about all consumed by furnaces in the State producing them. The great bulk of the Superior ores go to supply Illinois, Ohio, Pennsylvania and Eastern States, which require large quantities in addition to their own production. We give below the prices at which Lake Superior iron ore has been sold during the last seven years for season contracts, delivered at Cleveland and neighboring ports on Lake Erie.

GRADES.	1886.	1887.	1888.	1889.	1890.	1891.	1892.
Republic and Champion No. 1	$6.25	$7.00	$5.75	$5.50	$6.50	$5.50	$5.50
Cleveland and Lake Superior specular No. 1 . . .	5.50	6.50	5.25	5.00	6.00	5.00	5.00
Chapin and Menominee No. 1	5.25	6.00	4.75	4.50	5.50	4.25	4.25
Soft hematites, No. 1 non-Bessemer	4.50	5.00	4.00	3.75	4.50	3.75	3.75
Gogebic, Marquette, and Menominee No. 1 Bessemer hematites	5.00	6.00	4.75	5.00	6.00	4.75	4.50
Minnesota No. 1 Bessemer	5.75	6.75	5.75	5.50	6.50	5.50	5.65
Minnesota hard Bessemer hematite (Chandler) . .	. . .	. . .	. . .	. . .	. . .	. . .	4.85
Lake Superior and Lake Angeline extra low-phosphorus Bessemer	. . .	. . .	. . .	. . .	. . .	. . .	6.00

PIG IRON.

Sixty years ago the American blast furnace which would make four tons of pig iron in a day, or twenty-eight tons in a week, was doing good work. This year the maximum production of the world has been reached by Furnace I of the Edgar Thompson Steel Company, at Braddock, Pa., which made in January 12,706 gross tons, a daily average of 410 tons; best week 3,005 tons, best day 511 tons.

Nor has the growth of the industry been less remarkable than the individual capacities of the furnaces. In 1866 the United States had reached the production of Great Britian in 1835; that is to say she was then thirty-one years behind the latter country. At the end of 1884, she was but twenty-one years behind England. The prophecy was made by the Census Bureau in 1880, that, allowing for the same rate of increase for both countries, the United States will be fifteen years behind England in 1900, and will reach and surpass her in 1950, the production of pig iron in each country for that year, as determined from the equation of their respective curves, being a little over 30,000,000.

To the astonishment of the world, the United States recorded a growth unparalleled, and in 1890 surpassed England sixty years in advance of this prediction, producing $33\frac{1}{3}$ per cent. of the world's production. When it comes to consumption, we far out-strip any other, or any other two nations of the earth. We use probably as much iron as England, France and Germany taken together. Those countries depend largely on the export trade for their chief business.

Concerning the future, Hon. Abram S. Hewitt estimates that in 1900 the world will require 35,000,000 gross tons of iron, of which the United States must supply 45 per cent. Mr. Edward Atkinson estimates that if this accelerating demand should continue for the next eleven years, the supply must be 100 per cent. in excess of that which now prevails. In other words, the supply in 1900 will be 50,000,000 gross tons.

We consume more iron and steel *per capita* than any other country, our average consumption of these products being about three hundred and twenty pounds for every man, woman and child in the United States.

It would occupy too much space to enumerate the great diversity of uses to which iron and steel are put. As a means of power and force we see them in all stages, from the powerful engines and locomotives to the delicate hair spring of a watch; in domestic use in the furnaces and cooking utensils in every household; in art as displayed in the elaborate decorations and ornaments now used for beautifying our residences and public buildings.

The following statistics, compiled by the American Iron and Steel Association, will prove interesting as showing the extent of this industry:

BLAST FURNACE CAPACITY.

SUMMARY BY STATES.

STATES.	Furnaces Completed January, 1892.				Annual Capacity of Completed Furnaces, January, 1892, in net tons.			
	Anthracite.	Bituminous.	Charcoal.	Total.	Anthracite.	Bituminous.	Charcoal.	Total Net Tons.
Maine....	..	..	1	1	.....	.....	6,000	6,000
Massachusetts	..	..	4	4	.....	.....	19,500	19,500
Connecticut.	..	..	9	9	.....	.....	41,500	41,500
New York..	25	3	9	37	565,000	121,000	67,500	753,500
New Jersey.	15	..	..	15	274,345	.....	.....	274,345
Pennsylvania	124	80	15	219	2,742,848	3,858,200	61,700	6,662,748
Maryland...	..	5	8	13	.....	409,000	54,200	463,200
Virginia ..	..	19	14	33	.....	625,000	52,000	677,000
West Virginia	..	4	..	4	.....	184,000	.....	184,000
Kentucky...	..	7	3	10	.....	227,000	53,000	280,000
Tennessee...	..	13	6	19	.....	392,000	56,000	448,000
NorthCarolina	..	1	..	1	.....	6,000	.....	6,000
Georgia ...	..	2	4	6	.....	60,000	47,000	107,000
Alabama ..	..	38	15	53	.....	1,407,000	211,000	1,618,000
Texas.....	..	..	4	4	.....	.....	58,000	58,000
Ohio	..	60	12	72	.....	2,123,500	53,000	2,176,500
Indiana ...	..	2	..	2	.....	30,000	.....	30,000
Illinois ...	..	20	..	20	.....	1,365,000	.....	1,365,000
Michigan ..	..	..	23	23	.....	.....	436,000	436,000
Wisconsin..	..	4	6	10	.....	177,000	116,500	293,500
Minnesota..	..	1	..	1	.....	50,000	.....	50,000
Missouri ..	..	5	3	8	.....	175,000	47,000	222,000
Colorado ..	..	3	..	3	.....	100,000	.....	100,000
Oregon ...	..	..	1	1	.....	.....	15,000	15,000
Washington.	..	..	1	1	.....	.....	10,000	10,000
Total...	164	267	138	569	3,582,193	11,309,700	1,404,900	16,296,793

ROLLING MILLS, STEEL WORKS, ETC.
SUMMARY BY STATES.

STATES.	Rolling Mills and Steel Works...	Iron and Steel Rolling Mills.*...	Cut-nail Machines.	Steel Works. Bessemer.	Clapp-Griffiths.	Robert-Bessemer.	Open-Hearth.	Crucible.	Forges and Bloomaries.
Maine	1	1	..	..	..	..	..	..	..
New Hampshire	1	1	..	..	..	..	1	..	..
Massachusetts	14	13	326	2	1	..	2	1	..
Rhode Island	1	1	..	..	..	..	..	..	..
Connecticut	8	8	..	..	..	..	..	3	..
New York	23	19	..	1	..	..	4	4	9
New Jersey	20	19	193	..	..	..	3	6	3
Pennsylvania	211	192	1,555	18	3	1	38	24	14
Delaware	9	9	..	..	..	..	..	..	..
Maryland	6	6	..	1	..	..	..	1	2
Virginia	8	8	146	1	..	..	..	..	1
West Virginia	7	7	856	2	..	..	..	..	..
Kentucky	8	8	126	1	..	..	1	..	..
Tennessee	5	4	115	2	..	..	1	1	..
Georgia	1	1	..	..	..	..	..	..	..
Alabama	10	9	77	..	..	..	2	..	1
Texas	2	2	..	..	..	..	..	..	..
Ohio	59	56	1,215	6	..	..	10	2	..
Indiana	18	16	366	1	..	1	1	2	..
Illinois	26	23	398	8	1	1	6	..	..
Michigan	4	4	..	..	..	1	1	1	..
Wisconsin	2	2	..	1	..	..	..	..	..
Minnesota	2	2	..	..	..	..	..	..	..
Missouri	6	6	50	1	..	..	..	..	..
Iowa	1	1	..	..	..	..	..	..	..
Colorado	2	2	27	1	..	..	..	..	..
Wyoming	1	1	..	..	..	..	..	..	..
California	4	4	96	..	..	..	1	..	..
Total	460	425	5,546	46	5	4	71	45	30

*Excludes all steel works that contain no hot-rolling trains of rolls.

PRODUCTION OF PIG IRON BY STATES.

States—Net tons.	1890.	1891.	States—Net tons.	1890.	1891.
Pennsylvania .	4,945,169	4,426,673	Kentucky . .	53,604	50,225
Ohio	1,389,170	1,159,215	Missouri . . .	100,550	32,736
Alabama . . .	914,940	891,154	Connecticut .	22,552	24,428
Illinois	785,239	749,506	Texas	10,865	20,902
New York . .	369,381	352,925	Colorado . . .	23,588	20,290
Virginia . . .	327,912	330,727	Oregon	12,305	10,411
Tennessee . .	299,741	326,747	Massachusetts	5,531	10,069
Michigan . . .	258,461	238,722	Indiana . . .	16,398	8,657
Wisconsin . .	246,237	220,819	North Carolina	3,181	3,603
Maryland . . .	165,559	138,206	Minnesota . .		1,373
New Jersey . .	177,788	103,589	Maine	1,200	
West Virginia	144,970	96,637			
Georgia . . .	32,687	55,841	Total	10,307,028	9,273,455

SUMMARY IRON AND STEEL PRODUCTION.

Net Tons of 2,000 pounds, except nails.	1889.	1890.	1891.
Pig iron, including spiegeleisen	8,516,079	10,307,028	9,273,455
Spiegeleisen	85,823	149,162	143,098
Bessemer steel ingots	3,281,829	4,131,535	3,637,107
Bessemer steel rails	1,691,264	2,091,978	1,448,219
Open-hearth steel ingots	419,488	574,820	649,323
Open-hearth steel rails	3,346	4,018	6,589
Crucible steel ingots	84,969	79,716	81,297
Iron rails	10,258	15,548	9,229
Pig, scrap, and ore blooms	36,260	30,783	29,219
Kegs of iron and steel cut nails	5,810,758	5,640,946	5,002,176
Kegs of wire nails	2,435,000	3,135,911	4,114,385
Iron and steel wire rods	407,513	511,951	601,000
All rolled iron and steel, except rails .	4,160,491	4,634,076	4,573,841

STATISTICS. 71

Total Production of all Kinds of Steel from 1860 to 1891, in Gross Tons.

Years.	Gross Tons.	Years.	Gross Tons.	Years.	Gross Tons.
1860	11,838	1872	142,954	1882	1,736,692
1863	8,075	1873	198,796	1883	1,673,535
1864	9,258	1874	215,727	1884	1,550,879
1865	13,627	1875	389,799	1885	1,711,920
1866	16,940	1876	533,191	1886	2,562,503
1867	19,643	1877	569,618	1887	3,339,071
1868	26,786	1878	731,977	1888	2,899,440
1869	31,250	1879	935,273	1889	3,385,732
1870	68,750	1880	1,247,335	1890	4,277,071
1871	73,214	1881	1,588,314	1891	3,904,240

Production of Steel by the Different Processes.

Years.	*Bessemer. Net tons.	Open-Hearth. Net tons.	Crucible. Net tons.	Miscellaneous. Net tons.	Total.	
					Net tons.	Gross tons.
1885	1,701,762	149,381	64,511	1,696	1,917,350	1,711,920
1886	2,541,493	245,250	80,609	2,651	2,870,003	2,562,503
1887	3,288,357	360,717	84,421	6,265	3,739,760	3,339,071
1888	2,812,500	352,036	78,713	4,124	3,247,373	2,899,440
1889	3,281,829	419,488	84,969	5,734	3,792,020	3,385,732
1890	4,131,535	574,820	79,716	4,248	4,790,319	4,277,071
1891	3,637,107	649,323	81,297	5,022	4,372,749	3,904,240

* Bessemer column includes Clapp–Griffiths and Robert-Bessemer productions, these being simply a modification of the Bessemer process.

STEEL RAIL PRODUCTION.

Since 1874 our total production of Bessemer steel rails by Bessemer steel works and by rolling mills from purchased material has been as follows, in net tons:

Years—Net tons.	Pennsylvania.	Illinois.	Other States.	Total.
1874	66,902	48,280	29,762	144,944
1875	112,843	111,189	66,831	290,863
1876	203,750	133,713	74,998	412,461
1877	250,531	89,519	92,119	432,169
1878	308,093	143,785	98,520	550,398
1879	368,187	197,881	117,896	683,694
1880	495,716	257,583	201,161	954,460
1881	688,276	346,272	295,754	1,330,302
1882	759,524	336,122	342,509	1,438,155
1883	819,544	231,355	235,655	1,286,554
1884	763,223	290,185	63,213	1,116,621
1885	736,522	308,242	29,843	1,074,607
1886	1,111,171	430,975	221,521	1,763,667
1887	1,276,845	728,526	348,761	2,354,132
1888	930,140	488,639	133,852	1,552,631
1889	1,141,350	522,054	27,860	1,691,264
1890	1,470,490	587,537	33,951	2,091,978
1891	1,009,298	408,492	30,429	1,448,219

STATISTICS.   73

Average Monthly Prices of Iron and Steel.

MONTHS.	Old iron T rails, at Philadelphia.	No. 1X anthracite foundry pig iron, at Philadelphia.	Gray forge pig iron, at Philadelphia.	Gray forge pig iron, Lake ore, at Pittsburgh.	Bessemer pig iron, at Pittsburgh.	Steel rails, at mills in Pennsylvania.	Best refined bar iron, from store, Philadelphia.	All muck bar iron, at Pittsburgh.	Cut nails (base price), at Pittsburgh.
January, 1889	$23.50	$18.00	$15.50	$15.50	$16.75	$27.50	2.00c.	1.75c.	$1.90
February . .	23.50	18.00	15.25	14.75	16.35	27.50	1.90c.	1.70c.	1.90
March . . .	23.50	18.00	15.25	15.00	16.50	27.50	1.80c.	1.65c.	1.90
April	23.50	17.35	15.00	14.25	16.25	27.50	1.80c.	1.65c.	1.90
May.	22.75	17.00	14.75	14.00	16.00	27.00	1.85c.	1.60c.	1.85
June	22.50	17.25	14.90	14.00	16.00	27.50	1.90c.	1.60c.	1.85
July.	22.75	17.25	15.00	14.15	16.35	28.00	1.90c.	1.60c.	1.90
August . . .	23.50	17.50	15.25	14.90	17.50	28.00	1.95c.	1.72c.	1.90
September .	25.00	17.50	15.25	15.50	18.00	29.50	1.95c.	1.75c.	1.95
October . . .	26.00	17.50	15.60	16.60	20.75	32.00	2.00c.	1.80c.	2.25
November . .	26.50	18.50	16.75	17.25	21.75	34.00	2.05c.	1.80c.	2.25
December . .	27.25	19.25	17.25	18.25	23.75	35.00	2.15c.	1.90c.	2.30
January, 1890	27.50	19.90	17.90	18.00	23.60	35.25	2.20c.	1.90c.	2.40
February . .	27.25	19.50	17.38	18.00	22.55	35.00	2.20c.	1.90c.	2.35
March . . .	25.25	19.25	17.00	17.00	20.25	34.00	2.10c.	1.85c.	2.25
April	23.85	18.25	16.10	15.35	17.85	33.50	2.10c.	1.85c.	2.00
May.	23.25	18.00	15.65	15.25	17.55	31.35	2.10c.	1.75c.	1.90
June	24.50	18.00	15.50	15.25	19.00	31.50	2.00c.	1.80c.	1.95
July.	25.00	18.00	15.25	15.25	18.62	31.50	1.90c.	1.80c.	1.90
August . . .	25.00	18.00	15.10	15.25	18.10	31.25	1.95c.	1.85c.	1.85
September .	25.50	18.00	15.00	15.25	18.00	30.50	2.00c.	1.85c.	1.85
October . . .	25.50	18.00	15.00	15.00	17.35	30.00	2.00c.	1.85c.	1.85
November . .	25.10	18.00	15.00	15.00	17.00	29.00	2.00c.	1.85c.	1.80
December . .	24.50	18.00	15.00	14.75	16.60	28.50	2.00c.	1.85c.	1.80
January, 1891	23.50	17.50	14.50	14.25	15.95	29.00	2.00c.	1.80c.	1.65
February . .	23.35	17.50	14.50	14.50	16.25	30.00	1.90c.	1.75c.	1.65
March . . .	22.50	17.50	14.75	15.00	16.30	30.00	1.90c.	1.75c.	1.65
April	22.50	17.50	14.75	14.12	16.10	30.00	1.90c.	1.70c.	1.60
May.	22.00	17.50	14.75	14.00	16.50	30.00	1.90c.	1.70c.	1.55
June	21.00	17.50	14.75	14.00	16.25	30.00	1.90c.	1.70c.	1.55
July.	21.00	17.50	14.60	14.00	16.25	30.00	1.90c.	1.70c.	1.55
August . . .	21.50	17.50	14.50	14.00	16.00	30.00	1.90c.	1.70c.	1.55
September .	22.00	17.50	14.35	14.00	15.60	30.00	1.90c.	1.70c.	1.55
October . . .	22.00	17.75	14.35	13.85	15.50	30.00	1.85c.	1.70c.	1.60
November . .	21.75	17.50	14.25	13.50	15.15	30.00	1.85c.	1.68c.	1.55
December .	21.50	17.50	14.25	13.50	15.35	30.00	1.90c.	1.68c.	1.55
January, 1892	21.00	17.50	14.25	13.50	15.65	30.00	1.85c.	1.70c.	1.55
February . .	20.50	17.00	14.25	13.25	15.25	30.00	1.85c.	1.68c.	1.55
March . . .	20.25	16.50	14.00	13.00	14.75	30.00	1.85c.	1.62c.	1.50
April	20.00	16.00	14.00	13.00	14.50	30.00	1.90c.	1.60c.	1.50

World's Production of Iron and Steel.

COUNTRIES.	PIG IRON.		STEEL.	
	Years.	Tons.	Years.	Tons.
United States	1890	9,202,703	1890	4,277,071
Great Britain	1890	7,904,214	1890	3,679,043
Germany and Luxemburg	1890	4,637,239	1890	2,161,821
France	1890	1,970,160	1890	704,013
Belgium	1890	781,758	1890	239,266
Austria and Hungary	1890	925,308	1890	440,605
Russia, including Siberia	1890	745,872	1889	263,719
Sweden	1890	456,102	1890	169,286
Spain	1888	232,000	1888	28,645
Italy	1889	13,473	1889	157,899
Canada	1891	19,439	1889	24,887
Other countries, including Cuba	1891	80,000	1890	5,000
Total	...	26,968,468	...	12,151,255
Percentage of United States	...	34.1	...	35.2

World's Production of Iron Ore and Coal.

COUNTRIES.	IRON ORE.		COAL.	
	Years.	Tons.	Years.	Tons.
United States	1890	18,000,000	1889	126,097,779
Great Britain	1890	13,780,767	1890	181,614,288
Germany and Luxemburg	1890	11,409,625	1890	89,051,527
France	1887	2,579,465	1890	25,836,953
Belgium	1889	202,431	1890	20,343,495
Austria and Hungary	1890	2,200,000	1889	25,326,417
Russia, including Siberia	1888	1,433,513	1889	6,228,000
Sweden	1890	941,241	1890	258,000
Spain	1888	4,500,000	1888	1,203,119
Italy	1889	173,489	1889	390,320
Canada	1890	68,313	1890	2,783,626
Other countries, including Cuba	1890	2,000,000	1890	11,200,000
Total	...	57,288,844	...	490,333,524
Percentage of United States	...	31.4	...	25.7

STATISTICS.

PRODUCTION OF LEADING ARTICLES OF IRON AND STEEL IN THE UNITED STATES FROM 1880 TO 1891.

Statistics collected from the manufacturers by The American Iron and Steel Association.

Net tons of 2,000 pounds.

Products.	1880.	1881.	1882.	1883.	1884.	1885.	1886.	1887.	1888.	1889.	1890.	1891.
Pig iron	4,295,414	4,641,564	5,178,122	5,146,972	4,589,613	4,529,869	6,365,328	7,187,206	7,628,597	9,516,079	10,307,028	9,273,455
Spiegeleisen, included above	19,603	21,086	21,963	24,574	33,893	34,671	47,982	47,598	54,769	85,823	149,162	143,098
Bessemer steel ingots	1,203,173	1,539,157	1,696,450	1,654,627	1,540,595	1,701,762	2,541,493	3,288,357	2,812,500	3,281,829	4,131,535	3,637,107
Open-hearth steel ingots	112,953	146,946	160,542	133,679	131,617	149,381	245,250	360,717	352,036	419,488	574,820	649,323
Crucible steel ingots	72,424	89,762	85,089	80,455	59,662	64,511	80,609	84,421	78,713	84,959	79,716	81,297
Miscellaneous steel	8,465	3,047	3,014	5,598	5,111	1,696	2,651	6,265	4,124	5,734	4,248	5,022
Crude steel of all kinds	1,397,015	1,778,912	1,945,095	1,874,359	1,736,985	1,917,350	2,870,003	3,739,760	3,247,373	3,792,020	4,790,319	4,372,749
Bessemer steel rails	954,460	1,330,302	1,438,155	1,286,554	1,116,621	1,074,607	1,763,667	2,354,132	1,552,631	1,691,264	2,091,978	1,448,219
Open-hearth steel rails	13,615	25,217	22,765	9,186	2,670	4,793	5,255	19,203	5,261	3,346	4,018	6,589
Iron rails	493,762	488,581	227,874	64,954	25,560	14,815	23,679	23,062	14,252	10,258	15,548	9,229
Rails of all kinds	1,461,837	1,844,100	1,688,794	1,360,694	1,144,851	1,094,215	1,792,601	2,396,397	1,572,144	1,704,868	2,111,544	1,464,037
All rolled iron	2,333,668	2,643,927	2,493,831	2,348,874	1,937,397	1,804,526	2,283,622	2,588,500	2,411,654	2,586,385	2,820,377	} 6,037,678
All rolled steel									2,759,777	3,278,974	3,995,243	
Rolled iron, excluding rails	1,838,906	2,155,346	2,265,957	2,283,920	1,931,747	1,789,711	2,259,943	2,565,438	2,397,402	2,576,127	2,804,829	} 4,573,841
Rolled steel, excluding rails									1,201,885	1,584,354	1,829,247	
Kegs of cut nails and spikes	5,370,512	5,794,206	6,147,097	7,765,737	7,581,379	6,666,815	8,156,973	6,908,870	6,493,591	5,810,758	5,640,946	5,002,176
Blooms from ore and pig iron	74,589	84,606	91,293	74,758	57,005	41,700	41,909	43,306	39,875	36,260	30,783	29,219

THE A B C OF IRON.

GRAND SUMMARY.

IRON AND STEEL WORKS.	January, 1892.	November, 1889.
Number of completed Blast Furnaces—267 Bituminous, 164 Anthracite and Coke, and 138 Charcoal: total	569	573
Number of Blast Furnaces building—10 Bituminous and 1 Charcoal: total	11	27
Annual capacity of completed Blast Furnaces, net tons	16,296,793	13,168,233
Annual capacity of the Bituminous Furnaces, net tons	11,309,700	8,223,500
Annual capacity of the Anthracite Furnaces, net tons	3,582,193	3,723,333
Annual capacity of the Charcoal Furnaces, net tons	1,404,900	1,221,400
Number of completed Rolling Mills and Steel Works	460	445
Number of Rolling Mills and Steel Works building	18	11
Number of Single Puddling Furnaces (a double furnace counting as two single ones)	5,120	4,914
Number of Heating Furnaces	2,913	2,733
Number of Trains of Rolls	1,592	1,510
Annual Capacity of completed Rolling Mills, net tons	11,831,294	9,215,000
Number of Rolling Mills having Cut-nail Factories	65	75
Number of Cut-nail Machines	5,546	6,066
Number of Cut-nail Factories building	. . . . .	1
Number of Cut-nail Machines to be used in the new Factories	. . . . .	100
Number of Wire-nail Works	49	37
Number of completed standard Bessemer Steel Works	46	41
Number of Bessemer Steel Works building	2	. . . . .
Number of completed standard Bessemer Converters	95	88
Annual capacity (built and building) in ingots, net tons	6,560,000	5,600,000
Number of completed Clapp-Griffiths Steel Works	5	8
Number of Clapp-Griffiths Converters	9	14
Annual capacity in ingots, net tons	170,000	200,000
Number of completed Robert-Bessemer Steel Works	4	7
Number of Robert-Bessemer Steel Works building	. . . . .	1
Number of Robert-Bessemer Converters—6 completed and 2 partly built	6	11
Number of completed Open-Hearth Steel Works	71	56
Number of Open-Hearth Steel Works building—4 building and 1 standing nearly completed	4	5
Number of Open-Hearth Furnaces—164 completed, 7 building, and 7 standing nearly completed	164	116
Annual capacity (built and building) in ingots, net tons	1,550,000	1,200,000
Number of completed Crucible Steel Works	45	43
Number of Crucible Steel Works building	1	3
Number of Steel-melting Pots which can be used at each heat	2,934	3,378
Annual capacity in ingots, net tons	105,000	111,500
Number of Forges making wrought iron from ore	10	23
Annual capacity in blooms and billets, net tons	21,200	45,000
Number of pig and scrap iron Bloomaries	20	27
Annual capacity in blooms, net tons	36,000	44,000

RAILROADS.

The railroads are the largest factors in the consumption of iron and steel products. They annually consume in rails, bridges, cars and locomotives about one-half of the world's total production of iron and steel. We have built more miles of railroad than the whole of Europe, and have used in their construction as many rails, and in their equipment fully as many railroad cars and locomotives. At the close of 1889 the United States had twenty-five miles of railroad to every ten thousand of population, while Europe had a little more than four miles to the same population.

The following statistics are taken from the twenty-fifth annual number of "Poor's Manual of Railroads:"

MILEAGE OF UNITED STATES, 1891.

Mileage of railroads	167,845.56
Second tracks, sidings, etc.	46,683.39
Total track	214,528.95
Steel rails in track	174,775.14
Iron rails in track	39,753.81

ROLLING STOCK.

Locomotive engines	33,563
Cars—Passenger	23,083
Baggage, mail, etc.	7,368
Freight	1,110,286
Total revenue cars	1,140,737

MILEAGE.

Miles of railroad operated	164,261.91
Revenue train mileage—	
Passenger	320,712,013
Freight	493,541,969
Mixed	19,948,394
Total	831,203,376
Passengers carried	556,015,802
Passenger mileage	13,316,925,239
Tons of freight moved	704,398,609
Freight mileage	81,210,154,523

Statement Showing Assets and Liabilities of the Railroads of the United States.

ASSETS.

Cost of railroad equipment	$ 8,927,571,592
Real estate, stocks, bonds and other investments	1,588,590,522
Other assets	233,862,243
Current accounts	241,399,182
	$10,991,423,539

LIABILITIES.

Capital stock	$ 4,751,750,498
Bonds and debt	5,178,821,989
Unfunded debt	345,102,632
Current accounts	374,051,161
Total liabilities	$10,649,726,280
Excess assets over liabilities	341,697,259
	$10,991,423,539

RAILROAD MILEAGE—1830-1891.

POOR'S MANUAL.

Prior to 1827 all the railroads built were composed of wooden rails and constructed only for carrying heavy material very short distances. In 1827 the Baltimore & Ohio Railroad was chartered by the Maryland Legislature, and this was the first railroad opened for conveying passengers. It was opened for travel from Baltimore to Ellicott's Mills, a distance of thirteen miles, on May 24, 1830, and completed to Washington City August 25, 1834.

Years.	Miles in Operation.	Net Increase.	Years.	Miles in Operation.	Net Increase.
1830	23		1861	31,286	660
1831	95	72	1862	32,120	834
1832	229	134	1863	33,170	1,050
1833	380	151	1864	33,908	738
1834	633	253	1865	35,085	1,177
1835	1,098	465	1866	36,801	1,716
1836	1,273	175	1867	39,250	2,449
1837	1,497	224	1868	42,229	2,979
1838	1,913	416	1869	46,844	4,615
1839	2,302	389	1870	52,922	6,078
1840	2,818	516	1871	60,293	7,379
1841	3,535	717	1872	66,171	5,878
1842	4,026	491	1873	70,268	4,097
1843	4,185	159	1874	72,385	2,117
1844	4,377	192	1875	74,096	1,711
1845	4,633	256	1876	76,808	2,712
1846	4,930	297	1877	79,088	2,280
1847	5,598	668	1878	81,767	2,679
1848	5,996	398	1879	86,584	4,817
1849	7,365	1,369	1880	93,296	6,712
1850	9,021	1,656	1881	103,143	9,847
1851	10,982	1,961	1882	114,712	11,569
1852	12,908	1,926	1883	121,455	6,743
1853	15,360	2,452	1884	125,379	3,924
1854	16,720	1,360	1885	128,361	2,982
1855	18,374	1,654	1886	136,379	8,018
1856	22,016	3,642	1887	149,257	12,878
1857	24,503	2,487	1888	156,173	6,916
1858	26,968	2,465	1889	161,319	5,146
1859	28,789	1,821	1890	166,817	5,498
1860	30,626	1,837	1891	171,079	4,262

RAILROAD MILEAGE BY STATES.

The number of miles of railroad in each State and Territory of the United States at the close of 1891 is shown in the following table:

States.	Miles.	States.	Miles.
Maine	1,383.26	Louisiana	1,880.01
New Hampshire	1,144.88	Missouri	6,178.45
Vermont	1,001.99	Arkansas	2,304.95
Massachusetts	2,100.32	Texas	8,812.67
Rhode Island	223.48	Kansas	8,890.87
Connecticut	1,006.54	Colorado	4,441.33
New York	7,765.22	New Mexico Territory	1,423.82
New Jersey	2,132.41	Indian Country } Oklahoma Ter. }	1,272.08
Pennsylvania	8,919.98		
Delaware	320.12		
Maryland	1,269.44	Iowa	8,436.51
District of Columbia	20.66	Minnesota	5,670.88
Ohio	8,167.63	Nebraska	5,430.49
Michigan	7,187.44	North Dakota	2,222.77
Indiana	6,135.25	South Dakota	2,699.92
Illinois	10,189.38	Wyoming	1,048.71
Wisconsin	5,785.61	Montana	2,290.82
Virginia	3,573.64	California	4,484.63
West Virginia	1,547.11	Oregon	1,503.52
North Carolina	3,205.46	Washington	2,309.23
South Carolina	2,491.06	Nevada	923.18
Georgia	4,870.25	Arizona Territory	1,097.57
Florida	2,566.87	Utah Territory	1,335.66
Kentucky	2,962.45	Idaho	959.68
Tennessee	2,996.20		
Alabama	3,576.47		
Mississippi	2,440.39	Total	170,601.18

STATISTICS.

The *Manual* for the same year gives the proportion of railroad track in the United States which had been laid with steel rails and iron rails from 1880 to the end of 1891, as follows:

Years.	Miles of steel rails.	Miles of iron rails.	Total miles.	Per cent. steel of total.
1880	33,680	81,967	115,647	29.1
1881	49,063	81,473	130,536	37.5
1882	66,691	74,269	140,960	47.3
1883	78,491	70,692	149,183	52.7
1884	90,243	66,254	156,497	57.6
1885	98,102	62,495	160,597	61.0
1886	105,724	62,324	168,048	62.9
1887	125,459	59,588	185,047	67.7
1888	138,516	52,981	191,497	72.3
1889	151,723	50,513	202,236	75.0
1890	167,606	40,697	208,303	80.4
1891	174,775	39,754	214,529	81.4

In the above figures all tracks are included. In the period covered by the table the mileage of iron rails had decreased 50 per cent., while that of steel rails had increased nearly 400 per cent. Over 80 per cent. of our tracks is laid with steel rails.

HISTORY OF IRON IN ALL AGES.

Mr. Swank has very kindly given the author permission to extract from his work on the above subject interesting data concerning the early history and uses of iron, and we will conclude this work with a chapter under this head. Mr. Swank's book of over five hundred pages is so replete with the most interesting history of the processes, places, and persons identified with the iron industry, that the extracts, necessarily limited, give but little idea of the scope and detail of this most valuable contribution to iron literature. The work is almost indispensable to one who would familiarize himself with the inception and progress of the iron industry in this country. It not only preserves in chronological order a record of the beginning of the iron industry in every country, and in every section of our own country, but gives an individual history of all persons in any way intimately associated with its development.

EARLY HISTORY AND MANUFACTURE OF IRON.

The use of iron can be traced to the earliest ages of antiquity. Copper and bronze, or brass, may have been used at as early a period as iron, and for many centuries after their use began they undoubtedly superseded iron to a large extent, but the common theory that there was a copper or a bronze age before iron was either known or used is discredited by Old Testament history, by the earlier as well as the later literature of the ancient Greeks, and by the discoveries of modern antiquarians.

In his inaugural address as President of the Iron and Steel Institute, delivered in May, 1885, Dr. John Percy, the eminent English metallurgist, briefly considered the question whether iron was or was not used before bronze. He said: "It has always appeared to me reasonable to infer from metallurgical considerations that the age of iron would have preceded the age of bronze. The primitive method, not yet wholly extinct, of extracting iron from its ores is a much simpler process than that of producing bronze, and it indicates a much less advanced state of the metallurgic arts. In the case of iron all that is necessary is to heat the ore strongly in contact with charcoal; whereas, in the case of bronze, which is an alloy of copper and tin, both copper and tin have to be obtained by smelting their respective ores separately, to be subsequently melted together in due proportions, and the resulting alloy to be cast into moulds, requiring considerable skill in their preparation."

Iron was doubtless first used in Western Asia, the birth-place of the human race, and in the northern parts of Africa which are near to Asia. Most authorities admit that Tubal Cain, who was born in the seventh generation from Adam, was the inventor of the foundry. Geology tells us that castings may have been made before the times of Tubal Cain, but the evidence of bronze castings before the days of Tubal Cain are not plentiful and frequently are mere conjecture. He is described in the fourth chapter of Genesis as "an instructor of every artificer in brass and iron," and in the revised version as "the forger of every cutting instrument of brass and iron."

The Egyptians, whose civilization is the most ancient of which we have any exact knowledge, were at an early period familiar with both the use and the manufacture of iron, although very little ore has ever been found within the boundaries of Egypt itself. Herodotus tells us that iron tools were used in the construction of the pyramids. In the sepulchres at Thebes and Memphis, cities of such great antiquity that their origin is lost in obscurity, butchers are represented as using tools the colors of which lead antiquarians to conclude that they were made of iron and steel.

The reference to iron in Deuteronomy iv, 20, apparently indicates that in the time of Moses the Egyptians were engaged in the manufacture of iron, and that the Israelites were at least as familiar with the art as their task-masters. "But the Lord hath taken you and brought you forth out of the iron furnace, even out of Egypt."

A small piece of very pure iron was found under the obelisk which was removed from Alexandria to New York in 1880 by Commander Gorringe, of the United States Navy. This obelisk was erected by Thothmes the Third at Heliopolis about sixteen hundred years before Christ, and removed to Alexandria twenty-two years before the Christian era. The iron found under it was therefore at least nineteen hundred years old.

Iron is frequently mentioned in the story of the wanderings of the children of Israel. Canaan, the land of promise, is described by Moses, in Deuteronomy viii, 9, as "a land whose stones are iron." Iron is said to be still made in small quantities in the Lebanon Mountains. The manufacture was diversified, for we read of chariots of iron, agricultural implements and tools of iron. Axes, saws, and hammers of iron are mentioned during the reign of David. Isaiah speaks of harrows of iron, and in the tenth chapter, thirty-fourth verse clearly refers to axes, when he says, "and he shall cut down the thickets of the forest with iron."

The great strength of iron is frequently referred to in the Old Testament. In Psalms ii, 9, we read: "Thou shalt break them with a rod of iron," and in Psalm cvii, 10, we read of those who sit in darkness as "being bound in affliction and iron." Daniel says that "iron breaketh in pieces and subdueth all things."

In the Koran of Mohammed, fifty-seventh chapter, is found this sentence: "And we sent them down iron, wherein is mighty strength for war." The legend embodied in the note of the commentator to the first phrase is curious. It runs as follows: "That is, we taught them to dig iron from the mines. Al-Zamakshari adds that Adam is said to have brought down with him from the Paradise five things made of iron, viz.: an anvil, a pair of tongs, two hammers, a greater and a lesser, and a needle."

Steel also was made before the Christian era. Day says that in the British Museum are iron and steel tools, probably three thousand years old. Ages ago the city of Damascus manufactured its famous swords from Indian and Persian steel. Swords are still made at Damascus, but of inferior quality. The cutlers of India, however, now make the best of swords from native steel. George Thompson told Wendell Phillips that he saw a man in Calcutta throw a handful of floss silk into the air which a Hindoo cut into pieces with his sabre.

EARLY HISTORY OF IRON. 87

We have given references that are conclusive as to the early use of iron, but it is worthy of note, as affording additional proof, that the mythologies of both Greece and Egypt attribute the invention of manufacturing iron to the gods, thus showing the great antiquity of the art in both these countries.

The poems of Homer, written about eight hundred years before Christ, make frequent mention of iron. The art of hardening and tempering steel is fully described in the reference to the plunging of the fire-brand of Ulysses into the eye of Polyphemus, an act which is likened to that of the smith who "plunges the loud hissing axe into cold water to temper it, for hence is the strength of iron."

We follow the author on down through the Grecian period, viewing with wonder their proficiency in the use and skill in the manufacture of iron and steel and the art of metallurgy. After the lapse of twenty-five centuries, from this little island of Elba where the Greeks got all their ores when Rome was founded, we are receiving many cargoes annually. We can not linger with the author in his description of the battering-ram, the grappling-irons and the javelins of the Romans.

After the fall of Rome, Spain revived the iron industry, their catalan forges lighting up the forests of the Pyrenees in every direction. These catalan forges have been introduced into every civilized country of modern times, and still exist in almost their original simplicity in the mountains of both Spain and France, and even in the Southern States of our own country.

The modern blast furnace is supposed to have originated in the Rhine provinces about the beginning of the fourteenth century, but whether in France, Germany or Belgium, is not known. It is claimed by Landrin that there were many blast furnaces in France about 1450. Alexander states that in the latter half of the sixteenth century there was a blast furnace in the Hartz Mountains in Germany, which was twenty-four feet high and six feet wide at the boshes, built by Hanssien a Voightlander.

Blast furnaces were not introduced into England until the beginning of the fifteenth century. Prior to this, all iron made there was produced in catalan forges or high bloomaries directly from the ore and was, therefore, when finished, wrought or bar iron. John Ray, the naturalist, in 1672, describes in two papers appended to his "Collection of English Words," the blast furnaces and forges as they existed in England in his day. He got his account from one of the chief iron masters of Sussex, Walter Burrell, Esq., of Cuckfield, deceased.

THE MANNER OF THE IRON WORK AT THE FURNACE.

"The iron mine (ore) lies sometimes deeper, sometimes shallower, in the earth, from four to forty (feet) and upward. There are several sorts of mine—some hard, some gentle, some rich, some coarser. The iron masters always mix different sorts of mine together, otherwise they will not melt to advantage. When the mine is brought in, they take small-coal (charcoal) and lay a row of it, and upon that a row of mine, and so alternately

S. S. S., one above another, and, setting the coals on fire, therewith burn the mine. The use of this burning is to modify it, that so it may be broke in small pieces; otherwise if it should be put into the furnace as it comes out of the earth it would not melt, but come away whole. Care also must be taken that it be not too much burned, for then it will *loop*, i. e., melt and run together in a mass. After it is burnt they beat it into small pieces with an iron sledge, and then put it into the furnace (which is before charged with coals), casting it upon the top of the coals, where it melts and falls into the hearth, in the space of about twelve hours, more or less, and then it runs into a *sow*.

The hearth, or bottom of the furnace, is made of sand-stone, and the sides round, to the height of a yard, or thereabout; the rest of the furnace is lined up to the top with brick. When they begin upon a new furnace they put fire for a day or two before they begin to blow. Then they blow gently and increase by degrees 'till they come to the height in ten weeks or more. Every six days they call a *Founday*, in which space they make eight tun of iron, if you divide the whole sum of iron made by the foundays; for at first they make less in a founday, at last more.

The hearth, by the force of the fire, continually blown, grows wider and wider, so that at first it contains so much as will make a sow of six or seven hundred pounds weight; at last it will contain so much as will make a sow of two thousand pounds. The lesser pieces, of one thousand pounds or under, they call pigs.

Of twenty-four loads of coal they expect eight tuns of sow; to every load of coals, which consist of eleven quarters, they put a load of mine, which contains eighteen bushels. A hearth ordinarily, if made of good stone, will last forty foundays; that is, forty weeks, during which time the fire is never let go out. They never blow twice upon one hearth, though they go upon it not above five or six foundays. The cinder, like scum, swims upon the melted metal in the hearth, and is let out once or twice before a sow is cast.

THE MANNER OF WORKING THE IRON AT THE FORGE OR HAMMER.

In every forge or *hammer* there are two fires at least; the one they call the *finery*, the other the *chafery*. At the finery, by the working of the hammer, they bring it into *blooms* and *anconies*, thus:

The sow they, at first, roll into the fire, and melt off a piece of about three-fourths of a hundred weight, which, so soon as it is broken off, is called a *loop*. This *loop* they take out with their shingling tongs, and beat it with iron sledges upon an iron plate near the fire, so that it may not fall in pieces, but be in a capacity to be carried under the hammer. Under which they, then removing it, and drawing a little water, beat it with the hammer very gently, which forces cinder and dross out of the matter; afterwards, by degrees, drawing more water, they beat it thicker and stronger 'till they bring it to a *bloom*, which is a four-square mass of about two feet long. This operation they call *shingling the loop*. This done, they immediately return it to the finery again, and, after two or three heats and workings, they bring it to an *ancony*, the figure whereof is, in the middle, a bar about three feet long, of that shape they intend the whole bar to be made of it; at both ends a square piece left rough to be wrought at the chafery.

Note.—At the finery three load of the biggest coals go to make one tun of iron. At the chafery they only draw out the two ends suitable to what was drawn out at the finery in the middle, and so finish the bar.

Note.—1. One load of the smaller coals will draw out one tun of iron at the chafery. 2. They expect that one man and a boy at the finery should make two tuns of iron in a week; two men at the chafery should take up *i. e.*, make or work, five or six tun in a week. 3. If into the hearth where they work the iron sows (whether in the chafery or finery) you cast upon the iron a piece of brass it will hinder the metal from working, causing it to spatter about, so that it cannot be brought into a solid piece.

The English blast furnaces and refinery forges which have been described were counterparts of Continental furnaces and forges of the same period. The erection of the first coke blast furnace on the Continent of Europe was commenced in 1823, at Seraing, in Belgium, by John Cockerill, an Englishman by birth but a Belgian citizen, and completed in 1826, when it was successfully blown in. Other coke furnaces in Belgium and elsewhere on the continent soon followed. In 1769 an attempt to smelt iron ores by means of coke was made at Juslenville, near Spa, in Belgium, but without success.

One of the coke furnaces of the Hoerde iron works in Germany is said to have been continuously in blast from July 3, 1855, to May 29, 1874, or almost nineteen years.

The manufacture of pig iron with mineral fuel was greatly facilitated by the invention of a cylindrical cast-iron bellows by John Smeaton, in 1760, to take the place of wooden or leather bellows, and by the improvements made in the steam engine by James Watts, about 1769; both these valuable accessions to blast furnace machinery being used for the first time, through the influence of Dr. Roebuck, at the Carron iron works in Scotland. The effect of their introduction was to greatly increase the blast and consequently to increase the production of iron. The blast, however, continued to be cold at all the furnaces, both coke and charcoal, and so remained until 1828, when James Beaumont Neilson, of Scotland, invented the hot blast, which is now in general use in all iron-making countries. The origin of the rolling mill for rolling iron into bars, or plates, is not free from doubt. In 1783, Henry Cort, of Gosport, England, obtained a patent for rolling iron into bars with grooved iron rolls, and in the following year he obtained a patent for converting pig iron into malleable iron by means of a puddling furnace.

We find, however, that John Payne and Major Hanbury rolled sheet iron as early as 1728 at Pontypool, and patents were granted to other Englishmen before Cort's day. To the important improvements made by Cort, however, the iron trade of Great Britain is greatly indebted. With mineral fuel, powerful blowing engines, the puddling furnace, and grooved rolls Great Britain rapidly passed to the front of all iron-making nations.

Steel was largely made in England as early as 1609, and most probably in cementation furnaces, the product being known as blister steel and shear steel. The manufacture of steel by cementation, however, did not originate in England, but on the continent. In the year mentioned, John Hawes held the site of the Abbey of Robertsbridge in Sussex, upon which were eight steel "furnaces." The invention of crucible cast steel originated with Benjamin Huntsman, an English clockmaker, at Sheffield, in 1740, and not only Sheffield, the principal seat of its manufacture and of the manufacture of all kinds of cutlery, but all England as well was greatly profited by his discovery.

Percy says of the cementation process, by which until in late years most of the steel of Europe and America was produced: "This is an old process, but little is known of its history. According to Beckmann, there is no allusion to it in the writings of the ancients." Laudrin says: "Germany is also the first country where it was proposed to cement iron. Thence this art came to France, and was introduced at New Castle-on-Tyne, long before it was known at Sheffield, the present center of that fabrication." The word cementation is derived from the former use with charcoal of chemical compositions called cements, which were, however, not needed.

We have, in the preceding pages, traced the early uses and history of iron in the Old World, and will now review briefly its progress in this country.

In no other part of the American continent has the manufacture of iron ever risen to the dignity of a great national industry, and only in Canada of all the political divisions of North or South America outside of the United States has a serious effort been made to develop native iron resources. Indeed it is only in the northern latitudes in both hemispheres that iron is made in large or even noticeable quantities. This fact is only in part due to geological reasons. Climate and race tendencies have had much to do with the development of the metallurgical and all other productive industries in thè belt of the earth's surface above alluded to, and which may well be called the iron-making belt.

Foster, in his *Pre-historic Races of the United States of America,* says that "no implement of iron has been found in connection with the ancient civilization of America." He fully establishes the fact that the mound-builders manufactured copper into various domestic and war-like implements, but adds that the Indians of North America did not use copper in any form, although those of Central and South America did.

Prescott, the historian of the Conquest of Mexico and Peru, says that the native inhabitants of these countries, who were at the time of the conquest the most advanced in all the arts of civilization of the immediate predecessors of the white race in North and South America, were unacquainted with the use of iron, copper serving them as a substitute.

Our North American Indians were certainly unacquainted with the use of iron when the Spaniards, the English, the Dutch, and other Europeans first landed on the Atlantic coast. Stone was used, instead of metal, for their tools. The Rev. Dr. Joseph Dodridge expressed the opinion that "at the discovery of America, the Indians knew nothing of the use of iron. Any people who have ever been in the habit of using iron will be sure to leave some indelible traces of its use behind them; but the aborigines of this country have left none."

Professor Putnam, of Harvard University, the archæologist, found in the ancient mounds of Ohio masses of meteoric iron and various implements and ornaments made by hammering pieces of meteoric iron. This native iron the ancient people of Ohio used the same as they did native silver or native gold, simply as a malleable metal. None of the peoples, he is confident, understood smelting iron or in any way manufacturing it from iron ore. And it was only after contact with Europeans that the Indian tribes obtained iron in various forms, and in due time learned to heat it and shape it as a blacksmith would do.

To North Carolina belongs the distinction of first giving to Europeans the information that iron ore existed within the limits of the United States. The discovery was made in 1585 by the expedition fitted out by Sir Walter Raleigh and commanded by Ralph Lane, which made, on Roanoke Island, in that year, the first attempt to plant an English settlement on the Atlantic coast. Lane and his men explored the country along the Roanoke and on both sides from Elizabeth river to the Neuse. Thomas Harriot, the historian of the colony and the servant of Sir Walter, says that "in two places of the countrey specially, one about foure score and the other six score miles from the fort or place where wee dwelt, wee founde neere the water side the ground to be rockie, which, by the triall of a minerall man was founde to hold iron richly. It is founde in manie places of the countrey else; I know nothing to the contrarie but that it maie be allowed for a good marchantable commoditie, considering there the small charge for the labour and feeding of the men; the infinite store of wood; the want of wood and deerenesse thereof in England; and the necessity of ballasting of shippes."

No attempt was made to utilize this discovery, as the colonists were in search of gold and not iron. In 1586 they quarreled with the Indians and returned to England. Iron ore was not mined in North Carolina, nor was iron made within her boundaries until after many other colonies had commenced to make iron.

The first iron made from American ore was in the year 1608, and the ore came from Virginia. The vessel containing same sailed from Jamestown, and reached England May 20th. The ore was smelted and seventeen tons sold at £4 per ton to the East India Company.

The first attempt to make iron in this country was by the Virginia Company in 1619. The enterprise was located on Falling creek, a tributary of the James river, which it enters about seven miles below Richmond. The work of establishing the plant was deterred by the death of three of the master workmen, when, in 1621, John Berkley was sent over with his son and twenty experienced workmen. Before their completion, in March, 1622, in an Indian massacre Berkley and all his men were slain and the works destroyed. In 1624 the charter of the Virginia Company was revoked, and thus disastrously ended the first attempt of Europeans to make iron in America.

The first successful iron works were established in the province of Massachusetts Bay, not far from Lynn, between 1643 and 1645. The place was at that time called Hammersmith, after a place of that name in England, from which place several of the principal workmen came. Joseph Jenks prepared molds for the first castings that were made at Lynn. "A small iron pot,

EARLY HISTORY OF IRON.

capable of containing about one quart," was the first article cast at the furnace. This first iron utensil cast in this country is now in the possession of Messrs. Llewellyn and Arthur Lewis, of Lynn, who are the lineal descendants of Thomas Hudson, the first owner of the lands on Saugus river, on which the iron works were built, and who obtained possession of the pot immediately after it was cast.

With the exception of the blast furnace, which was slowly developed from the high bloomary, and of the cementation process for producing steel, which doubtless originated during the period when the blast furnace was developed, no important improvements in the manufacture of iron and steel occurred from the revival of the iron industry in Europe about the beginning of the eighth century until we reach the series of improvements and inventions in the eighteenth century, a period of a thousand years.

It is about one hundred years since Henry Cort prominently brought the rolling mill and the puddling furnace to the attention of the iron-making world, and scarcely a hundred and fifty years since coke was first successfully used in the blast furnace, and steel was first made in England in crucibles.

Since Huntsman's invention, which still gives us our best steel, there have been many other improvements in the manufacture of steel, and more recently there has been a very great relative increase in its production and use as compared with iron, until it has become a hackneyed expression that this is the Age of Steel. While this is true in the sense that steel is replacing iron, it is well to remember that the ancients made steel of excellent quality, and that the art of manufacturing it was never lost, and has never been neglected. The swords of Damascus, and the blades of Toledo bear witness to the skill in the manufacture of steel which existed at an early day in both Asia and Europe. German steel was widely celebrated for its excellence during the middle ages, and steel of the same name, and made by the same process, still occupies an honorable place among the metallurgical products. Even Huntsman's invention of the art of making the finest quality of steel in crucibles, while meritorious in itself, was but the reproduction and amplification in a modern age of a process for manufacturing steel of equal quality which was known to the people of India thousands of years ago.

The ancient and the early European processes for the manufacture of both iron and steel do not compare unfavorably with those of modern times in the quality of the products they yielded. Modern processes excel those which they have replaced more in the uniformity and quantity of their products than in their quality.

In the present age, mechanical skill of the highest

order unites with the subtle operations of the chemist to produce iron and steel in such quantities, and with such uniformity of product, as to amaze the student of history, the political economist, the practical statesman, and the man of all wisdom.

INDEX.

	PAGE.
Iron—What Is It?	7
Pig Iron—An account of Blast Furnace Process	11
Constituents of Iron	20
Carbon in Cast Iron	21
Silicon in Cast Iron	24
Phosphorus in Cast Iron	29
Manganese in Cast Iron	31
Sulphur in Cast Iron	35
Numbering of Iron	37
Analyses	41
Grading of Iron	43
How to Reduce Cost of Mixture	46
Steel—Description of Several Processes	49
Physical Properties of Metals Defined	55
Shrinkage of Castings	56
Weights of Castings from Patterns	57
Table of Tenacities and Resistances	58
Formula for Mending Castings	59
Test for Sulphur in Coke	59
Iron Ores—How Classified	61
" Statistics	62–65
Pig Iron—Growth of Manufacture	66
" Consumption per Capita	67
" Blast Furnace Capacity	68
" Production by States	70

	PAGE.
Steel—Production	70
" Production of each Variety	71
Steel Rail Production	72
Iron and Steel—World's Production	74
Iron Ore—World's Production	74
Coal—World's Production	74
Production of Leading Articles in Iron and Steel	75
Grand Summary	77
Railroads—Mileage	77
" Rolling Stock	77
" Assets and Liabilities	78
" Mileage by Years	79
" Mileage by States	80
" Miles of Iron and Steel Rails	81
Early History and Manufacture of Iron	83–99

Classified Business Directory.

IRON ORE.

	PAGE.
PICKANDS, BROWN & CO.	116
PICKANDS, MATHER & CO.	116

COKE.

L. E. OVERMAN & CO.	115

COKE AND COAL.

L. E. OVERMAN & CO.	115
GEO. H. HULL & CO.	107
E. B. BLANDY	118

COPPER.

CRAMER & BURT	105

STEEL.

E. B. BLANDY	118

IRON AND STEEL FOUNDERS.

THE CONGDON BRAKE SHOE CO.	108

FOUNDRY SUPPLIES.

S. OBERMAYER & CO.	109
MILLINGTON WHITE SAND CO.	104
CHICAGO FOUNDRY SUPPLY CO.	113
DETROIT FOUNDRY EQUIPMENT CO.	111
F. B. STEVENS	116

CUPOLAS, CRANES, ETC.

PAGE.
DETROIT FOUNDRY EQUIPMENT CO.... 111

FOUNDRY PUBLICATIONS.

THE IRON AGE.......................... 114
THE FOUNDRY 110
HISTORY OF IRON IN ALL AGES 112

PIG IRON.

CRAMER & BURT......................... 105
PICKANDS, BROWN & CO................. 116
GEO. H. HULL & CO..................... 107
FOSTER, BACKMAN & HAWES ..op. Title Page.
E. B. BLANDY... 118
PICKANDS, MATHER & CO. 116
DUNHAM, KEEDY & CO................... 104
IROQUOIS FURNACE CO......... op. Title Page.
GAYLORD IRON CO....................... 108
PENINSULAR IRON CO.................... 113
OHIO IRON AND STEEL CO. 106
PINE LAKE IRON CO..................... 104
F. B. STEVENS 116

BLAST FURNACES.

OHIO IRON AND STEEL CO..... 106
IROQUOIS FURNACE CO......... op. Title Page.
PENINSULAR IRON CO................... 113
GAYLORD IRON CO....................... 108
PINE LAKE IRON CO..................... 104

PINE LAKE IRON COMPANY,
"Champion"
LAKE SUPERIOR CHARCOAL PIG IRON,

No. 655 THE ROOKERY,

R. M. CHERRIE, President.
H. C. DOLPH, Treasurer.

CHICAGO, ILL.

A. H. DUNHAM.   D. V. KEEDY.

DUNHAM, KEEDY & CO.,

Pig Iron,

939 Rookery,   CHICAGO.

———— TELEPHONE 695. ————

MILLINGTON WHITE SAND CO,

SAND FOR
IRON AND STEEL WORKS,
ARCHES, CUPOLAS,
FURNACES,
FINE CASTINGS,
LOCOMOTIVE AND
PLASTERERS' SAND.

OFFICE:
126 WASHINGTON STREET,
ROOM 43,

CHICAGO.

MINE AT MILLINGTON, KENDALL COUNTY, ILLINOIS.

AMBROSE CRAMER. CHARLES S. BURT.

CRAMER & BURT

PHENIX BUILDING,

CLARK AND JACKSON STREETS,

Chicago, Ill.

Pig Iron,

    Ingot Copper,

        Sheet Copper,

            Spelter,

                Iron Ores,

                    Wire Rope.

THOS. H. WELLS, President.
JOHN C. WICK, Vice-President.

F. H. WICK, Treasurer.
R. BENTLEY, Sec'y and Gen'l Mgr.

MARY FURNACE

THE
Ohio Iron & Steel Co.

LOWELLVILLE, OHIO,

MANUFACTURERS OF PIG IRON.

SPECIALTY:

AMERICAN SCOTCH FOUNDRY IRON,
BRAND, MARY OHIO SCOTCH.

OFFICE OF

THE OHIO IRON & STEEL CO.

Believing the trade will be interested in the great progress made in producing in the United States a Foundry Iron in every respect equal to the Imported Scotch, we give herewith comparative analyses of four well-known brands of Imported Scotch and our No. 1 Mary Ohio Scotch Foundry Iron. We challenge comparison of these analyses. Many inferior Irons are to-day being put on the market and called "Ohio Scotch" Foundry, and in many cases have been sold to our customers with intent to deceive.

Please ask for "Mary Ohio Scotch," and see that you get it; and demand an analysis with every order, if you are in doubt.

Respectfully,

THE OHIO IRON & STEEL CO.,
LOWELLVILLE, OHIO.

No. 1 MARY OHIO SCOTCH.

Metallic Iron	92.01
Silicon	3.15
Graphite	2.97
Combined Carbon	.25
Phosphorus	.425
Sulphur	.018
Manganese	1.20
	100.023

IMPORTED SCOTCH.

	Colt-ness.	Glengar-nook.	Curn-brae.	Laug-loan.
Metallic Iron	91.34	91.800	90.65	92.177
Silicon	2.93	2 021	2.93	1.68
Graphite	3.14	2.147	2.90	2.99
Comb. Carbon	.40	.880	.76	.75
Phosphorus	.628	1.121	1.12	.642
Sulphur	.048	.037	.03	.021
Manganese	1.08	1.915	1.51	1.74
Copper			.04	
Titanium			.06	
	99.566	99.921	100.00	100.00

AGENTS:

Pickands, Brown & Co., Chicago, Ill.

Pickands, Mather & Co., Cleveland, Ohio.

N. S. Bartlett & Co., Boston and New York.

(106)

PIG IRON.   COKE.

GEO. H. HULL & CO.,

LOUISVILLE, KY.

BRANCHES:

44 WALL STREET,
NEW YORK.

201 EAST GERMAN STREET,
BALTIMORE.

22 LACLEDE BUILDING,
ST. LOUIS.

555 THE ROOKERY,
CHICAGO.

CORRESPONDENCE SOLICITED.

We are specially prepared to help out founders who are having trouble with their mixtures.

Our aim is to furnish only material of superior quality.

GAYLORD IRON CO.,

MANUFACTURERS OF

Lake Superior Charcoal Pig Iron

DETROIT, - - MICH.

Special attention given to the manufacture of Iron for malleable purposes.

The Congdon Brake Shoe Co.
IRON & STEEL FOUNDERS

GENERAL OFFICES: SUITE 1016 MONADNOCK BLDG. CHICAGO.

FOUNDRIES: C & E. I. RR. & 59TH ST.

THE LARGEST AND MOST RELIABLE FOUNDRY SUPPLY HOUSE IN THE WORLD.

THE S. OBERMAYER COMPANY,

CINCINNATI, OHIO,

MANUFACTURERS

Foundry Facings,

India Silver Lead

and Plumbago,

AND GENERAL

FOUNDRY SUPPLIES AND EQUIPMENTS,

Molders' Tools, Fire Brick, Cupola Blocks, Etc.

We keep in stock and MANUFACTURE everything needed in a Brass or Iron Foundry (except metal and fuel).

WRITE FOR CATALOGUE.   *No Charge for TRIAL Samples.*

THE FOUNDRY

A MONTHLY TRADE JOURNAL,

Published on the Tenth of each Month and Devoted to the Interests of the whole

Foundry Business.

THE RECOGNIZED ORGAN OF THE

STOVE, BENCH, MACHINERY, STEEL, CAR AND BRASS FOUNDRY INTERESTS.

TECHNICAL ARTICLES

On the mixing, melting and the most improved methods of molding and pouring metals of all kinds, by the most able writers on Foundry subjects, will be found, from time to time, in its columns.

Every Foundry Proprietor, Superintendent, Foreman, Molder, Melter and Core-maker should take it if he desires to keep abreast of the times.

Subscription Rates,   -   - $1.00 per year.
Single Copies,   -   -   -   10 cents.

Clubs of eight or more may have "The Foundry" mailed to their addresses for seventy-five cents per year.

THE FOUNDRY PUBLISHING COMPANY,

172 Griswold Street,   DETROIT, MICH.

DETROIT FOUNDRY EQUIPMENT CO.

OFFICE AND WORKS : Cor. Michigan Avenue and D. & B. C. R. R.
CHICAGO : 62 West Jackson Street.   NEW YORK : 47 Cedar Street.

MANUFACTURERS OF

THE WHITING PATENT CUPOLA.

An Established Success !   In use all over the Country !   Made in Twelve Sizes !
The Most Economical and Substantial Cupola Made !

CRANES.
Jib and Traveling.   Hand and Power.

LADLES.
Geared, Hand and Reservoir Ladles of all Sizes and Capacities.

Tumblers, Trucks, Sand Sifters, Foundry Elevators, Etc.

Sole makers of **WHITING'S PATENT CAR WHEEL FOUNDRY SYSTEM**
and complete Foundry Outfits. Write for Estimates.

HISTORY
OF THE
Manufacture of Iron in All Ages,

AND PARTICULARLY IN THE UNITED STATES FROM COLONIAL TIMES TO 1891.

ALSO A SHORT HISTORY OF EARLY COAL MINING IN THE UNITED STATES, AND A FULL ACCOUNT OF THE INFLUENCES WHICH LONG DELAYED THE DEVELOPMENT OF ALL AMERICAN MANUFACTURING INDUSTRIES,

By JAMES M. SWANK,

Secretary and General Manager of The American Iron and Steel Association for Twenty Years, from 1872 to 1892.

In One Volume, Royal Octavo, 574 Pages, Large Type, Good Paper, Well Printed, Best Cloth Binding, Gilt Title.

SECOND EDITION, THOROUGHLY REVISED AND GREATLY ENLARGED.

Sold Only at the Office of the American Iron and Steel Association.

PRICE, SEVEN DOLLARS AND FIFTY CENTS.

I now offer to Iron and Steel Manufacturers, the officers of Public Libraries and others, a second edition of this work in a handsome volume of 574 pages, including 132 pages of historical details not found in the first edition. The whole book has been printed from new type.

It is respectfully suggested, in order to save correspondence, that orders for the History be accompanied by checks or money orders, payable to my order. The book will be forwarded promptly, encased in a paper box. It will be sent at my cost for expressage or postage, and care will be taken that it be received in good condition. It is now ready for delivery.

Address. **JAMES M. SWANK,**

No. 261 South Fourth Street, PHILADELPHIA, PA.

T. H. EATON, President. ROBERT LEETE, Vice-Pres't.
SOLON BURT, Sec'y and Treas.

THE PENINSULAR IRON CO.

MANUFACTURERS OF

Charcoal Pig Iron

FOR CAR WHEEL, MALLEABLE AND FOUNDRY USE,

FROM LAKE SUPERIOR ORES,

DETROIT,   -   -   MICH.

Peerless Facing Mills.

Our manufactures are **Peerless** in all that this word implies. Specialists and Experts in the manufacture of such materials as will aid in producing the **Finest, Brightest and Smoothest Castings.**

PARTICULAR ATTENTION PAID TO STOVE PLATE AND RETURN FACINGS.
We are originators of the best STOVE PLATE FACINGS now in use.

DIRECT IMPORTERS AND REFINERS OF

Silver Leads, Graphite or Plumbago,
FOUNDRY FACINGS, BLACKINGS AND FOUNDRY SUPPLIES.

IRON AND BRASS FOUNDRIES COMPLETELY EQUIPPED.
No Charge for Trial Samples. Send for Illustrated Catalogue and Price List.

THE CHICAGO FOUNDRY SUPPLY CO.,   -   **CHICAGO, ILL.**

THE IRON AGE.

A Review of the Hardware, Iron and Metal Trades.

PUBLISHED WEEKLY, SEMI-MONTHLY AND MONTHLY.

The position of THE IRON AGE is indicated in these facts:

It has for thirty-eight years been a leader among trade journals, and is the representative paper of the Iron and Steel, Hardware and Metal interests.

It has grown from a four-page sheet, with few advertisements, until its weekly issue contains from forty-five to sixty pages of reading matter, and from one hundred to one hundred and fifty pages of advertisements.

Its editorial contents have kept pace with the progress of manufacture and the needs of the trade, each issue having important illustrated articles, special contributions, telegraph and cable advices, etc.

It circulates in all parts of the country and in foreign lands, having a greater circulation at home and abroad than the combined circulation of all of its competitors.

The reason for its great circulation is, that without regard to expense the publisher endeavors to make the paper useful to its readers, adding new features as the need or opportunity may suggest.

SUBSCRIPTION RATES.

Weekly Edition, issued every Thursday morning,   -   **$4.50 a Year.**

Semi-Monthly Edition, first and third Thursdays, with the Hardware Bulletin for the second, fourth and fifth Thursdays,   -   -   -   -   .   -   **2.30 a Year.**

Monthly Edition, first Thursday in the month, with the Hardware Bulletin for the second, third, fourth and fifth Thursdays,   -   -   -   -   -   -   **1.15 a Year.**

L. E. OVERMAN.   W. J. COOK.

L. E. OVERMAN & CO.,

138 JACKSON STREET,

PHENIX BUILDING,   CHICAGO,

GENERAL SALES AGENTS FOR THE

McClure Coke Co.

PITTSBURGH, PA.,

AND SHIPPERS OF THE HIGHEST GRADES OF

Pennsylvania, Ohio, Indiana and Illinois

COALS.

The product of the McClure Coke Co.'s ovens is **exclusively** from the famous **Connellsville vein of Coal,** and is of the **highest standard of excellence for Foundry purposes** (for which they burn 72-hour coke **only**), and for Blast Furnace use. The makers of the highest grades of iron and steel produced in the world are using the "McClure" Coke, because of its evenness and reliability. We gladly quote delivered prices, and will make every effort to fulfill the wishes of consumers of Coke, if they will tell us of their wants.

L. E. OVERMAN & CO.,

138 Jackson St., Phenix Building,

CHICAGO.

HERE is a little girl who has just realized that her doll is stuffed with saw-dust. Many a man realizes the same fact too late in life to recoup. To keep out of the saw-dust of business worry and annoyance, take care in buying. The subscriber carries an extensive line of **Pig Iron** suitable for any mixture, **Facings** and **Blackings** of superior quality, **Fire Brick, Cupola Blocks, Molding Sand**—our own pits—and a complete line of Shovels, Riddles and Brushes. In short, we are in the **Foundry Supply** business.

F. B. STEVENS,
74 Griswold Street,
WAREHOUSE:
11 and 13 Atwater Street West.
DETROIT, MICH.

PICKANDS, BROWN & CO.,
PIG IRON AND IRON ORE,

1007, 1009 AND 1011 ROOKERY BUILDING,
CHICAGO.

PICKANDS, MATHER & CO.,
Pig Iron Department.

Western Reserve Building, CLEVELAND, OHIO.

WHEELER FURNACE COMPANY.

When you get this

Imprint on your Lithographing or Printing

We'll guarantee the work has been well done—

It's good.

We are thoroughly equipped. Our work is as good as that of the best houses in the United States.

When you need anything in our line — Fine Lithographing, Wood or Process Engraving, Printing, Binding, Electrotyping— let us give you an estimate. You will find our prices reasonable, and our work FIRST CLASS. Our address is 334-338 West Green Street, Louisville, Ky.

Pig Iron   Steel

STRUCTURAL IRON AND STEEL.

Blooms

E. B. BLANDY,
201
EAST GERMAN ST.,
Baltimore, - Md.

Billets

Correspondence Solicited for
All Kinds of IRON and STEEL PRODUCTS,
CAR WORKS and RAILROAD SUPPLIES.

Iron Ore   Coke

www.ingramcontent.com/pod-product-compliance
Lightning Source LLC
Chambersburg PA
CBHW020136170426
43199CB00010B/772